AF476896

"
TALK OF THE
CITY
A HISTORY OF
NORWICH CITY
IN 1000 QUOTES
"

"TALK OF THE CITY

A HISTORY OF NORWICH CITY IN 1000 QUOTES

DAVID CUFFLEY

First published by Pitch Publishing, 2015

Pitch Publishing
A2 Yeoman Gate
Yeoman Way
Durrington
BN13 3QZ
www.pitchpublishing.co.uk

A CIP catalogue record is available for this book
from the British Library.

ISBN 978 178531-035-5

Typesetting and origination by Pitch Publishing

Printed by Bell & Bain, Glasgow, Scotland

Contents

Acknowledgments

I WOULD like to thank my former employer, Archant Norfolk, publisher of the *Eastern Daily Press* and *Norwich Evening News*, for permission to quote from its publications.

I am especially grateful to Rosemary Dixon, librarian at Archant, for her assistance in trawling the newspaper archives for Norwich City material.

To Keith Skipper, who has followed the Canaries as a lifelong fan and distinguished football writer, a heartfelt thank you for writing a marvellous foreword.

I am indebted to Roger Harris, Keith Whitmore and Kasper Wikestad for kindly providing the photographs that appear in these pages.

Special thanks go to George Nobbs for permission to use extracts from *Keelan: The Story of a Goalkeeper*, to Bryan Gunn for use of quotes from his autobiography, *In Where It Hurts*; and to Bruce Robinson for extracts from his book, *Passing Seasons*.

Credit is due to soccer historians Dick Middleton and Mike Davage for years of meticulous research tracking down ex-Canaries, many of whom became the subject of interviews that provided extracts included here.

Finally, a tribute to the Norwich City footballers, managers, directors, supporters and reporters over more than a century who provided the inspiration for this volume, either with their stirring deeds on the field or their words of wisdom, folly, joy, despair, passion and humour off the pitch.

David Cuffley

Foreword by Keith Skipper

THE BEST quote I was ever offered in my seasons as a Canary scribe was a couple of quid for helping a player fill in a highly complicated form in respect of an insurance claim.

With no other takers at the back of the team bus – and the manager snoozing near the front – I accepted that little windfall with relish and thanks for a useful grammar school education.

Let me emphasise immediately that the life of a football reporter was rarely as straightforward or lucrative as that. When I started with the arrival of Ron Saunders at Carrow Road in 1969, I eschewed a growing habit of overloading match reports and reflective articles with fatuous quotes from managers or players.

Same with tittle-tattle in the national press…an occasional grain of wholesome wheat in mountains of speculative chaff. Remember, too, how Norwich's geographical position and 'country cousins' tag left them untroubled by Fleet Street newshounds for long periods at a time before they started rubbing shoulders with the big boys on a more regular basis.

Running reports in the *Pink 'Un* on Saturday afternoons and in-depth analysis in the *Eastern Daily Press* and *Evening News* on the Monday dominated coverage. There was no local radio, no website and no social media to spread facts, opinions and rumours, while television interest was largely confined to Anglia's *Match of the Week* highlights after Sunday lunch.

One of the biggest challenges of my Carrow Road tenure was acclimatising to a dramatic change in managerial personality and style about halfway through. Ron Saunders, dour and dogmatic, gave way to John Bond, all colour and controversy.

While one threw a protective shield around his players, and confined himself to startling comments along 'we gave 110 per cent' lines, the other courted the media shamelessly and encouraged everyone within reach to wear bleeding hearts on sleeves.

They had nothing in common other than being born within a few weeks of each other in 1932 and both joining Manchester City to further their careers and leave Norwich with the sort of 'stepping stone' complex Paul Lambert reinforced in more recent years.

Saunders would not accept the 'hardman' label although he did confess to being 'a bit of a swine'. Perhaps the distinction had to rest somewhere in that old proverb about making silk purses out of sows' ears. He produced a promotion team out of material few people considered suitable for a history-making journey.

His style was bound to hurt in some cases. I recall winger Steve Grapes exclaiming after a gruelling stint on the training beat, 'He makes bloody Hitler look like Edith Cavell!'

It is also claimed the no-nonsense manager made one player feel so inadequate that the poor creature dug a hole in which to hide – and then did extra training because he took too long to dig it.

While his successor settled for a far more entertaining and open regime, he often needed protection from a nonstop passion to oblige. Cynical operators chasing juicy headlines for national tabloids made him a regular target – but the 'Bondwagon' kept on rolling. I devised a weekend format designed to restore a measure of calm and balance to a scene dominated by regular doses of Saturday teatime fever. With the dust settled and the main agitators returned to the capital, I then asked Mr Bond for his more considered opinions on a quiet Sunday afternoon.

I'm sure several of my successors on the Canary beat, David Cuffley among them, have shared the challenge to temper a fiercely parochial spirit with a drop or two of chilling honesty so as to stay true to themselves and thousands of Norwich City followers with reason to trust what they read in the local papers.

This excellent compilation of telling quotes from Canary history, passionate, witty, brutally frank, playfully obtuse, conjure up so many pictures of memorable characters and unforgettable fixtures.

For old codgers like me, the stirring FA Cup run of 1958/59 still provides inspiration, consolation – and determination not to join so many others in the dug-out of despair when it comes to the future of this grand old game.

That run to within sight of Wembley's gates came just two years after an appeal had been launched to keep Norwich City alive. The dream of becoming the first Third Division side to reach a final ended with Billy Bingham's goal in a tense semi-final replay against Luton at St Andrew's in Birmingham.

The journey home had every right to be soaked in tears of bitter disappointment. For some, however, it transformed into a magnificent outburst of defiance and togetherness. City players trooped from one compartment to another on the Top Brass Special, a railway phenomenon that blossomed during the campaign, chanting, 'You sang for us, now we'll sing for you!'

That must be my favourite line from the entire Norwich City ledger, not so much a quote as the forging of a precious new union between players and supporters. They really were in it together with one of the most poignant singalongs in soccer history as 'On The Ball, City!' scaled fresh heights of fervour.

I know now that gripping chapter in Carrow Road folklore was part of my apprenticeship for a media career, including long spells of trying to make sense of sport in general and football in particular.

**Keith Skipper,
Cromer, 2015**

Introduction

I CLEARLY remember one of the first pieces of advice I was given when I started reporting on the fortunes of Norwich City nearly 30 years ago, 'Not too many lunar orbits or poorly tropical birds, please.'

This was the 1980s and it was a reference to the trend in post-match interviews for victor and vanquished to describe themselves, respectively, as 'over the moon' or 'sick as a parrot'.

There are various explanations for the origins of those phrases. The first has its most likely roots in a nursery rhyme that dates back 250 years. The second is also said to be centuries old, but is credited in more recent times to the former Liverpool defender Phil Thompson. Appropriate, you may think.

I was being warned, politely, to avoid phoning over the same old clichés when following up the traditional match report with the instant reaction of those involved. 'Have you got the quotes?' was the cry from a clutch of anxious reporters trying to do three things at once in the frantic first half-hour after the final whistle, as they compared notes and rushed to file their stories before the next deadline.

Among those hastily gathered words of wisdom from players, managers and even the occasional match official there was always the chance of eliciting the memorable one-liner or classic comment that would be remembered for years to come.

Today's journalists and broadcasters could be forgiven the occasional grimace every time they hear that it is a 'steep learning curve', that every other match is 'huge' or 'massive', or that this is a 'must-win game'. As opposed to the games you simply must lose, perhaps? Or, worst of all, in the wake of a fearful drubbing, to be told yet again by the poor unfortunate nominated to meet the press that he and his team-mates have to 'take the positives'.

But we have reason to be grateful that despite the advent of media training, there are still footballers who are less guarded, more spontaneous and can give vent to their true feelings and innate sense of humour, and that there will always be those individuals – players, managers and fans – who stand out from the crowd on good days and bad because they are articulate, original, self-deprecating, even poetic or simply very funny.

Former City manager John Bond was a dream for the media because he had an opinion on everything and was never afraid to voice it. Always entertaining, many of his observations and predictions from seven years at Carrow Road are reproduced here, some of them prophetic and one or two that were rather wide of the mark, notably about seeing out his nine-year contract – he left two years after signing it – and the claim that with a few more players like Drazen Muzinic he could win the league title.

Bond's predecessor at Carrow Road, Ron Saunders, was a man of fewer words but when he spoke they were no less pertinent. There is little in this book more withering and to the point than his observation at Wembley, after steering Aston Villa to victory in the League Cup Final over Bond's Canaries, 'I am unable to smoke big cigars like some managers.'

I was fortunate enough to interview more than 20 Norwich City managers, former managers or caretaker bosses in nearly 30 years working on the sports desk of the *Eastern Daily Press* and *Norwich Evening News*, plus literally hundreds of players and past players, opponents, directors, supporters, broadcasters, referees and the odd celebrity fan.

Fresh from the glory of the Canaries' wonderful Championship play-off final win at Wembley, it is perhaps a paradox that the greatest triumphs do not necessarily produce the greatest interviews.

In much the same way that bad news very often sells more newspapers – or earns more hits on a website – than good news, so it is that some of the best-remembered quotes come from difficult or unhappy times for Norwich City, rather than days of great celebration or prosperity, and from unpopular managers or chairmen as opposed to crowd or media favourites.

The fans' disillusionment over the sale of star centre-forward Ron Davies to Southampton for a knock-down £60,000 in 1966 brought out terrace humour at its best after full-back Alan Black became new manager Lol Morgan's first signing for a more modest £9,000. With apologies to Los Bravos, up went the chant, 'Black is Black, we want Ron Davies back.'

Everyone remembers Robert Chase's assertion in 1994 that if striker Chris Sutton was sold before the start of the next season, the chairman would also be on his way out of Carrow Road – he was constantly reminded of it during the extra two years he stayed in office as the team that impressed so many in Europe was swiftly dismantled and the club dropped out of the Premier League and plunged into a financial crisis.

Nigel Worthington achieved notable success in saving City from relegation in 2001, taking them to the play-off final in 2002 and promotion to the Premier League as Football League champions two years later.

But arguably his best remembered quote came in 2006, just a few matches before he was dismissed, when he lambasted his team in a radio interview for throwing away a 3-1 lead at Southend by having 'a flick, fart and a fanny'.

Glenn Roeder may have felt he was attempting a joke at the club's 2008 annual meeting at Carrow Road when he told a critical shareholder, 'Sorry, I must have missed your tenure as England manager.' But the comment backfired badly and arguably hastened his exit, with dissatisfaction among fans and poor results contributing to his sacking two months later.

But what comes through these pages too, I hope, is very much the humour, the passion and the spirit of those on the inside – the players, managers, directors and officials – and those looking on, the supporters, reporters and broadcasters.

Within these pages you can find out, if you have forgotten, the identity of Tweedledum and Tweedledee, the Milk Tray man, Albert Tatlock and the Red Devil, who also happened to be the manager on 'gardening leave' with no garden. And you can discover which ex-Canary claimed he was turfed out to pay for the club's undersoil heating.

I hope you enjoy the selection and here's to more memorable Talk of the City as they return to the Premier League.

David Cuffley

Some Things are Better Left Unsaid

'If I had three or four more like him I could start talking about winning the First Division.' **(John Bond hails Drazen Muzinic's debut against Southampton, September 1980)**

'He had a pretty good scoring record against us when he was at Liverpool. It would be nice to think that he could be scoring for us.' **(Ken Brown signs striker David Fairclough, February 1985)**

'If Chris Sutton is not here at the start of next season, neither will I be.' **(Chairman Robert Chase, who promptly sold Sutton for £5m but stayed in office for two more years, 1994)**

'The really good players only start to play in February and March. That's when cup competitions and league titles are decided.' **(Manager John Deehan, 1994, before a run of one win in 20 Premier League games relegated City)**

'Mark is happy to continue working hard for Norwich City and trying to win a first-team place. For my part, I'm happy to bring him back into the first-team squad.' **(John**

Deehan, 24 hours before Mark Robins is sold to Leicester, January 1995)

'I am hoping that sooner rather than later results on the pitch will entice those who are staying away from Carrow Road back to the ground.' **(Martin O'Neill, eight days before resigning as manager, December 1995)**

'Norwich are sensibly running a tight ship. Chase has taken hard decisions now rather than when the club might have become overstretched.' **(David Miller, 1995)**

'Now we've got a win under our belts we can concentrate on what is, effectively, a 20-game league.' **(City boss Gary Megson gets his first win at Sunderland to move into the top six in the First Division, January 1996)**

'The lads think we are more suited to playing with two wide men in midfield.' **(Mark Bowen leaves himself stranded on 399 City appearances by questioning manager Gary Megson's tactics, 1996)**

'Now we can relax a bit and build for next season. Everyone's been getting a bit anxious recently.' **(Mike Walker on the 5-0 home win over Swindon, April 1998, five days before being sacked)**

'The future for the club looks really exciting. I'm delighted to be part of it and to be able to help deliver the Norwich City vision.' **(Bob Cooper becomes a City director, 1998)**

'We're delighted to welcome Bob Cooper on to the board. His footballing knowledge will be of enormous benefit.' **(City chairman Barry Lockwood, 1998)**

'At the back end of 1997/98 we tried out the stilt-walkers and clowns with a reasonable amount of success. We have decided to concentrate the clowns where the kids are so we're looking for entertainment for the adults.' **(City communications manager Steve Greenall discusses pre-match entertainment, 1999)**

'We've got Bryan Hamilton, who is regarded as one of the best coaches in the world.' **(City chairman Bob Cooper, 1999)**

'Our plans for the Academy are ambitious. We want it to become the technical centre of this country.' **(Bob Cooper, 1999)**

'He's tall, very quick and got a beautiful left foot.' **(City boss Bryan Hamilton on £225,000 Dutch signing Raymond de Waard, March 2000)**

'Bryan Hamilton was my first choice right from the very beginning. I just lost out on the vote.' **(Delia Smith, May 2000)**

'Nigel Worthington has been fantastic. I'm very pleased with the way he's settled in.' **(City boss Bryan Hamilton, August 2000, four months before Worthington replaced him as manager)**

'We've got high hopes because we've been playing well recently and scored six goals in our last two away games. We have sometimes conceded sloppy goals but I'm sure we will not do that on Sunday.' **(Mathias Svensson, 48 hours before a 6-0 defeat at Fulham relegates City, May 2005)**

'It is going to be an experience that will shape lives for years to come. Hopefully it will be an "I was there then" moment to tell the grandchildren about, not an open wound that will weep and fester for years to come.'

(Columnist Man in the Stands, the day before the 6-0 defeat at Fulham)

'If we're all pushing in the right direction I'm sure it will be a joyful ride and hopefully one of these days we'll be saying fasten your seatbelts and let's go, let's get going back to the Premier League.' **(Peter Grant becomes City manager, October 2006)**

'Peter Grant is absolutely clear he wants to win the Championship and that is also our objective as a board.' **(City director Andrew Turner, 2007)**

'I'm very pleased to be given the opportunity to get back into Championship football. I'll be working for a very good club and manager and look forward to helping get Norwich City Football Club back into territory that it's more familiar with.' **(City goalkeeping coach Stuart Murdoch arrives, then leaves four days later, January 2008)**

'Pablo Counago recommended Norwich to me. He said it was a top club and a nice city to live in. He gave it his full recommendation.' **(City signing Juan Velasco before the first of his three games for the Canaries, 2008)**

'I'm glad the season is over and we're not relegated. Leicester have gone down and they've spent millions. Leeds went down not so long ago so it proves it can happen to anyone.' **(Defender Gary Doherty, a year before Norwich followed suit, May 2008)**

'I think our supporters are going to like all of our signings. I know it's taken a long time to bring them to the club, but anyone can sign five or six bad players in one day, then five or six bad players the next day. There are hundreds of bad players out there looking for clubs.' **(Glenn Roeder, July 2008)**

'We can most definitely challenge for promotion. I wouldn't have come here if I'd have thought otherwise. I spoke to the gaffer when I came here and he had the same sort of plans and I want to be part of that.' **(New signing Sammy Clingan in positive mood, July 2008)**

'I want people to look at me coming out of the training ground or coming out of Carrow Road and think "Fotheringham looks like a Premier League player".' **(Skipper Mark Fotheringham, July 2008)**

'Sorry, I must have missed your tenure as England manager.' **(Glenn Roeder to a critical shareholder at club's annual meeting, November 2008)**

'Let's stop living in the past – let's move on. I would make the same decision today. Football is all about opinions. And the bottom line is that the football opinion that counts at this football club at this moment in time is mine.' **(Glenn Roeder defends his decision to release Darren Huckerby, annual meeting, November 2008)**

'The lads here, the boys on loan as well, should feel privileged to play for this team because there have been some great players down the years played for Norwich. And a guy with Bryan Gunn's experience, it's not bad having a guy like that in charge here.' **(Mark Fotheringham, February 2009, three weeks before Gunn dropped him for good)**

'I still think we'll be all right. It's a good side out there and I think we've got the right credentials to get out of trouble. There are going to be nervy moments, we aren't going to win 12 on the trot but I think we have enough and it's important we all believe that.' **(Striker Jamie Cureton forecasts Championship survival, February 2009)**

'I come from a winning mentality and that's what we need here at Norwich to get ourselves back up. I suppose Aussie mentality is all about winning and that's what football is about. I look forward to setting new goals and achieving them with this club.' **(Goalkeeper Michael Theoklitos signs for City, July 2009)**

'I believe Micky Theoklitos has got character and that's the reason I brought him to the club. I've never seen him let seven goals in before.' **(Manager Bryan Gunn, August 2009)**

'I think that it is massive that to be a winning team you don't get too hung up on results that don't go your way. At Exeter we got hammered at home to Chesterfield 6-1.' **(Midfielder Matthew Gill, speaking just before his debut, the 7-1 home defeat by Colchester)**

'The Norwich board have acted appallingly towards our club recently and I'm sure I have never wanted to win a game of football so badly.' **(Colchester chairman Robbie Cowling before his side's 5-0 home defeat by Norwich, 2010)**

'I've always felt I was good enough to play in the Premier League and I'm just delighted it's all been sorted now. I'm just really looking forward to getting on the pitch and showing everyone what I can do next season.' **(Jacob Butterfield signs for City, July 2012, but never makes a Premier League appearance)**

'I cannot wait to play my first game for Norwich. I am really happy about having the chance to play in the Premier League, it is brilliant for me personally and for my career.' **(Striker Luciano Becchio signs from Leeds, January 2013)**

'Ricky's profile is a perfect fit for us – he's young, ambitious and a proven goalscorer.' **(Manager Chris Hughton confirms signing of £8.5m striker Ricky van Wolfswinkel, 2013)**

'I played a few games against English clubs in the Europa League and scored against English teams so I know what I have to do and I know what I can do in the Premier League. It is the only competition I really wanted to play in.' **(Ricky van Wolfswinkel signs from Sporting Lisbon, 2013)**

(2)

The Way We Were

'A meeting of those interested in football matters in the city will be held at the Criterion Café, White Lion Street, on Tuesday next, to consider the advisability of forming a Norwich City Club. You are formally invited to attend.' **(Joe Nutchey and Robert Webster issue a circular, June 1902)**

'The great difficulty at first was to persuade the delegates that there was a place called Norwich.' **(City chairman Wilfred Burgess applies to the Southern League, 1905)**

'It would be like renting a shop, stocking it and preparing for business and someone else having the run of the place for five and a half days a week.' **(City chairman John Pyke rejects the terms for a new lease for Newmarket Road, 1908)**

'It was the happiest club I have ever known and the directors were the finest lot of people I had ever met.' **(Percy Varco, 1920s centre-forward)**

'Tricky Hawes was an ostler who looked after the horses. If a player got injured on the field he would trot up the field to the player. If he gave the player a massage it was performed as though he were massaging a horse, with a soothing noise to calm the animal down.' **(Pre-war player Bernard Robinson recalls the trainer's unorthodox methods)**

'Aye, I remember The Nest all right. What a ground that was. There was a slope of about eight feet from one end of the pitch to the other, and there was a great concrete wall at one end, just a few feet from the touchline. The players had to be careful of bumping into that.' **(Full-back Archie Campbell)**

'It should never have been a football ground and I was glad to get away from the place – it was a wicked ground.' **(Bernard Robinson recalls The Nest)**

'I would rather train young players to my own ideas than spend a fortune on buying new men who don't know how we play at Norwich.' **(Manager Tom Parker, 1935)**

'There is a grave possibility of The Nest being declared unsuitable.' **(Billy Hurrell, City chairman, warns of an impending ground move, May 1935)**

'We always used to stay at the best hotels and I remember that our manager, Tom Parker, used to take us to stay at the Pier Hotel, Gorleston, on the Friday night before a home game.' **(Bernard Robinson)**

'The King was in Norwich for the opening of the new City Hall building. My father was Lord Mayor at the time. And it was his suggestion that the King visit the game.' **(Geoffrey Watling recalls King George VI watching City v Millwall, 1938)**

'During my last leave from the Army I was asked for trials at Norwich. I was demobbed on the Saturday, playing for the reserves on Tuesday and making my debut at Northampton the following Saturday.' **(Goalkeeper Ken Nethercott)**

'I remember when he jumped, he seemed to jump higher than the crossbar and he had this ability to hang in the air. He was one of the greats of that era.' **(Ken Nethercott recalls facing Tommy Lawton, 1948)**

'Dancing after Wednesday night is strictly forbidden except when special permission is given…any players using licensed premises after Monday night unless special permission is given will be severely dealt with by the directors.' **(Players' rule book, 1950s)**

'There was nothing at all down one side of the pitch and the cricket stand was about 100 yards away. The only other place I remember like that was the County Ground at Northampton.' **(Terry Allcock on playing at Bramall Lane, Sheffield)**

'He was a very nice man. He always talked to you if the action was at the other end. A real gentleman.' **(*Eastern Daily Press* photographer Dick Jeeves on goalkeeper Ken Nethercott)**

'We were both based in the north of England so we decided to hire a removal lorry and move to Norfolk together to save a bit of money.' **(Terry Allcock remembers joining City from Bolton at the same time as Blackpool's Derrick Lythgoe)**

'I am the last person to think I can't make mistakes. Any manager makes them.' **(Archie Macaulay, 1961)**

'We were a good side and we played lovely football, so much so that the Third Division was a bit of a doddle the year after the FA Cup semi-final. But it was a bit tougher in the Second Division and I don't think we were on a par with the present team.' **(City giantkiller Jimmy Hill)**

'Archie Macaulay was such a great tactician and a great motivator. The other side were always rubbish and you felt ten feet tall when you took the field.' **(Full-back Bryan Thurlow)**

'It's hard to realise that a life's ambition has been achieved.' **(Skipper Ron Ashman on promotion to the Second Division, 1960)**

'It was the home game against Southend, when we won 4-3 to clinch promotion, when I think I was really accepted by the crowd because I scored one goal and made two more.' **(Winger Bill Punton wins over the fans, 1960)**

'I got married in the morning and had to rush straight from the church to get the train to Brighton where we were playing. I hardly remember anything about the game. It was all too much for me that day, but it was all arranged before the move.' **(Forward George Waites has a fixture clash, February 1961)**

'Four years ago we were a struggling Third Division side. We might have dropped into the fourth had we not done so well in my first season as manager. To me, our achievement of keeping in the Third Division was almost as great as any of the others of the last four years.' **(Archie Macaulay, 1961)**

'Archie Macaulay used to do his team talks with pennies on the table. He didn't use a blackboard but he would put a handful of coins on the table and move them into position to show us what he wanted to do.' **(Bunny Larkin)**

'Players make mistakes but I consider the Norwich City players have done a great job of work for the club over the past four years.' **(Archie Macaulay defends his team, October 1961)**

'In my first year, my instructions were to see that we remained in the Third Division. In certain quarters it was thought that if we achieved this it would be a miracle. We finished eighth. After that, it was a question of consolidation in the Third Division. We made an indifferent start, then finished fourth. The following year it was "we want promotion". It wasn't easy but we did it. Then it was consolidation again. We finished fourth, the highest place the Canaries have held in their history.' **(Archie Macaulay defends his record, one match before resigning as manager, October 1961)**

'I want to know the players and how they tick. That has always been my policy.' **(Willie Reid becomes manager, December 1961)**

'The bottle landed near Gerry Mannion and myself and in all innocence he threw the bottle back and hit a kid in the head. I don't think he even thought about what it was. It was terrifying. I've played in European football and for Newcastle against Rangers and Celtic, and that day at Grimsby is one of the most frightening things I have seen. The players were glad to get off the pitch at the end.' **(Ollie Burton recalls crowd trouble at Grimsby, September 1962)**

'George Swindin was the best manager I ever played for and my career was up and down after he left. When George got us going we were a good side with a lot of talent.' **(City forward Jim Oliver)**

'With this increased accommodation, I am hoping the powers that be will allocate one or two matches to Norwich in the World Cup of 1966.' **(City Supporters' Club secretary Stan Springall, 1962)**

'That goal celebration picture? I know the one you mean, with my arms raised. It was on show in Pilch's sports shop and that was the first time my wife set eyes on me, on that picture in the shop window.' **(Jim Oliver's hat-trick against Stoke, 1963, brings an unexpected bonus)**

'It's nice to know we have such capable reserves and we appreciate the way they rose to the occasion on Saturday. I've had a chat with Oliver, Conway and Miller and naturally they are disappointed.' **(City manager Ron Ashman leaves out three forwards after a 6-0 home win over Stoke, March 1963)**

'Barry was more than just a Norwich City player. He was part of the club and the position he occupied, both on and off the field, can never be re-filled.' **(Chairman Geoffrey Watling pays tribute on the death of club captain Barry Butler in a road accident, April 1966)**

'I'm not a defensive-minded man. I feel players must realise that they are entertainers and that we have got to sell the game a little more to the public. I think players sometimes tend to forget this.' **(Lol Morgan is appointed manager, June 1966)**

'There were pictures in the dressing room at Old Trafford of me and Heathy kissing the boot, but everyone on the picture, they were all smoking. Everyone had a cigarette in their hand, but of course, you wouldn't see that today.' **(Gordon Bolland recalls the FA Cup win at Old Trafford, 1967)**

'Sideburn'd and mustachio'd, they will force Beethoven and Pancho Villa to look to their laurels. Perhaps "new wave" is not a bad description after all.' **(Bruce Robinson on City's changing hairstyles, 1968)**

'Michael and his dad and I walked all the way along the river to the ground. It was standing only in the River End. I fell in love with Graham Paddon and his blond hair swaying around in the wind. Then I got very upset when he went to West Ham.' **(Delia Smith)**

'This year we have given the club £40,000 and they used it very well to buy a centre-forward, David Cross.' **(City Supporters' Club secretary Stan Springall, 1972)**

'It's a good job this was only a bust and not a full frontal.' **(Chairman Geoffrey Watling is presented with a sculpture of himself, February 1973)**

'Me and John Miller, the winger who signed from Ipswich, used to go to college two afternoons a week to do a hairdressing course. Then a friend, Chris Chapman, gave me my first job in hairdressing when I had to pack up the game.' **(Former defender Paul Kent)**

'The Leeds manager was Jimmy Armfield, who played at Blackpool with my dad. There was a knock on the dressing room door and he came in to have a word with me. He had seen the name Lythgoe on the teamsheet and came in for a chat about my dad.' **(Phil Lythgoe makes his third appearance for City as a teenager, 1978)**

'I imagine there will be one or two transistors in the church. The one good thing is I'll be in just the right place to pray for a Norwich victory.' **(A family wedding means chairman Sir Arthur South misses the crucial last game of the season, 1981)**

'You were very understanding of my situation as I had a young family growing up in Wilmslow, Cheshire, so you allowed me, fixtures permitting, to train on a Monday and Tuesday with either the sun bed king, Ron Atkinson, at Manchester United or with Joe Royle at Ice Station Zebra, otherwise known as Oldham Athletic.' **(Asa Hartford pens Ken Brown an 80th birthday message)**

(3)

Goals Galore

'If the game had gone on for another ten minutes I'd probably have had three or four more.' **(Leslie Eyre scores five goals in a 7-2 FA Cup win against Brighton, 1956)**

'Dick Turpin never made a more successful ride.' **(*Evening News* match report as Bunny Larkin dashes to York to score twice on his City debut, 1960)**

'It was one of those days when everything I did came off. I could do no wrong.' **(Jim Oliver on his hat-trick in a 6-0 home win against Stoke, 1963)**

'Many of his scoring headers were initiated so far out from the goal that if the camera was pointing at the goalmouth then Davies himself would not be in the picture.' **(Bruce Robinson on Ron Davies, *Passing Seasons*)**

'I was under a lot of pressure because Norwich had sold Ron Davies to Southampton for quite a bit of money in those days. Getting a hat-trick on my debut against Derby, I was almost joint top scorer after one game.' **(Centre-forward Laurie Sheffield, another 1966 hat-trick hero)**

'I had scored 12 league goals before I got injured in January and Ken Foggo only overtook that with his 13th when he scored in the last but one game at Orient when we clinched promotion.' **(City striker Peter Silvester on the knee injury that sidelined him for two years)**

'Graham Paddon took a long throw and they headed it out and I was going to run back into the defence because I thought I'd better get back quick, but I stayed in and it went back to Graham who got it on his left foot and crossed it in. Big Frank Burrows, the centre-half for Swindon, just got underneath it and as soon as that ball came over his head, I knew I was going to score. No goalkeeper could have saved that header – it went right up into the junction.' **(Duncan Forbes describes his vital goal against Swindon, 1972)**

'There was a lot of hype about the match being our first game and everything and Everton were a top side. It wasn't a particularly spectacular goal but it was very, very good for me to score the first goal for the club in the first match having just been promoted.' **(Jim Bone scores City's first goal in the First Division, 1972)**

'I remember it well. John Connolly cut in on his left foot and crossed it. It was a far-post header and I was all over Duncan Forbes – the great legend that was Duncan. When I joined Norwich years later, he constantly reminded me that I had fouled him, but I said, "Read the paper, Duncan, it was 1-1."' **(Joe Royle recalls his goal for Everton, which spoiled City's First Division debut, 1972)**

'It must have been the final minute when we won a corner on the right and Max Briggs took it. I was so tired I was only just arriving in the penalty area as the ball came over – it was like one continuous run. Duncan Forbes spun the keeper and took him out and I was able to power a header in.' **(Dave Stringer on his late winner against Crystal Palace, 1973)**

'Millwall just had time to kick off before the referee blew the whistle, but John Bond had left the stand and was going towards the dressing room. When we got back he started to give us a rollicking, saying how could we lose to Millwall. But he didn't realise we had scored. He couldn't believe it when they told him I'd scored – the only goal in my Norwich career. He changed his tone then because he had been ready to lace into us.' **(Geoff Butler scores an injury-time equaliser at The Den, 1975)**

'I scored with a diving header, which was something, and that was my second goal for the club. I suppose it was my first really significant input into the team because it was a very important goal.' **(Mick McGuire scores in a 3-0 promotion-clinching win at Portsmouth, 1975)**

'It was a volley and it went in for a change. Queens Park Rangers had a good side with people like Gerry Francis, Stan Bowles and Dave Thomas but we did them that day.' **(Peter Morris saves his first City goal for his last home game for the club, 1976)**

'Perhaps after this Mike Smith will play me in the forward line.' **(Centre-half David Jones, overlooked by the Wales manager, scores twice at West Ham, 1977)**

'I still remember all my three goals. They were all away, at Middlesbrough, Birmingham and Everton. I had just four short years as a professional. The knee's still a bit of a disaster but I'd do it all again.' **(Midfielder Billy Steele)**

'To go 3-0 down in the first 20 minutes – you don't forget that. You think, "What have I let myself in for?" But we fought back to 3-3 and we really should have won it.' **(Keith Robson scores on his debut against First Division leaders Nottingham Forest, 1978)**

'I had no right shooting and I would have got a right volley from my father had it gone up into the stand, instead of which it hit the back of the net.' **(Kevin Bond scores a long-range special against Leeds, August 1979)**

'The goal was special, but then so are Liverpool. No matter what pressure they are under, they always try to come back at you.' **(Justin Fashanu on his BBC Goal of the Season, February 1980)**

'Yes, I've got to admit, I got a fiendish satisfaction from scoring against them knowing Bond was watching. I reckon we had a few scores to settle and this was definitely one in my favour. It was nice to do it in such an important match.' **(Midfielder Mick McGuire scores in a 2-0 win over John Bond's Manchester City, April 1981)**

'Scoring in seven games in a row was some sort of record so I was very proud of that.' **(Striker Ross Jack on his 1981 goal spree)**

'I've still got two more league matches to go, if selected, and if Norwich want me after that I'll be delighted. If not, I will have enjoyed my time here and I'll know I haven't let them down.' **(New signing Mick Channon scores the winner for the second home game in a row, against Swansea, January 1983)**

'There was no time to think but where the ball dropped just seemed like a dream to me and after I had poked the ball into the net it still didn't seem real.' **(Louie Donowa scores a late equaliser against Manchester United, 1983)**

'You didn't know I had the pace, did you?' **(Robert Rosario scores a spectacular FA Cup goal at Huddersfield, 1987)**

'It's something you cannot forget – the day you score your first goal. It is an unbelievable feeling, up with the very best.' **(Jeremy Goss scores against Chelsea, 1987)**

'Goal of the Season was awesome because only one person a year wins it.' **(Robert Rosario wins ITV Goal of the Season award for scoring against Southampton, 1989/90)**

'It was a complete disaster, wasn't it? I've played in some bad matches and seen some bad performances in my time here, and this kind of thing happens from time to time. But we were beaten by a side who absolutely slaughtered us. After the first 20 minutes we fell apart. The headline which said we were slaughtered was dead right.' **(Manager Dave Stringer digests a 6-2 home defeat by Nottingham Forest, January 1991)**

'It was the first time I'd got into the box in the entire game and I thought if it broke down I'd be struggling to get back so I'd better put the ball in the net. It's a goal I'll never forget.' **(Everton fan Colin Woodthorpe scores for City in a 3-0 home win against Liverpool, February 1992)**

'I usually manage one goal for each of my clubs and to score against Liverpool, I was delighted, as an Everton supporter.' **(Defender Colin Woodthorpe, 1992)**

'I'm not best pleased but I couldn't have done anything better for myself than to score a hat-trick. At least I've left them something to remember me by.' **(Darren Beckford scores three in a 4-3 win against Everton, March 1992, but faces suspension for the FA Cup semi-final)**

'I can't ask for anything better than that. I suppose the pressure is on me now to keep that form up. It was the first match and it's important I don't get carried away.' **(Striker Mark Robins comes off the bench to score twice on his debut, a 4-2 Premier League win at Arsenal, August 1992)**

'I managed to chip David Seaman for the fourth goal. Doing that to an England goalkeeper is something you will always remember.' **(Mark Robins, August 1992)**

'It's an unbelievable experience to see the birth of your son, and to score the winner tonight is tremendous.' **(John Polston has a double celebration after a 1-0 Premier League win over Aston Villa, 1993)**

'It was a very important penalty to take. I had a gut feeling that Mike Hooper thought I'd just blast it down the middle, so I hit it low to his left-hand side.' **(David Phillips scores the winner against Liverpool, 1993)**

'What's that worth then, Mr Chairman?' **(Andy Linighan scores Arsenal's FA Cup winning goal and indirectly puts City into Europe for the first time, 1993)**

'The last one was up there as one of the most satisfying goals I ever scored because I had to do everything very quickly. Players very often have to do things when there is not much time and space and it brings the best out of your natural ability.' **(Efan Ekoku scores four times in a 5-1 win at Everton, September 1993)**

'If you make the right run, nine times out of ten Ian Crook will find you and when he chipped it back over the defence it was perfect.' **(Efan Ekoku scores City's first goal in European football against Vitesse Arnhem, 1993)**

'I think it came off my knee and went in from about a yard. But I soon had to run back because I had a hell of a nosebleed.' **(Full-back Ian Culverhouse scores against Everton in 1994, one of only two goals for City)**

'It was a wet day. I put my left foot down and it gave way and I hit the ball with my right and it took a ricochet off my left foot and spun up in the air and went past Tim Flowers into the top right-hand corner. It was one of those freak goals you don't get very often.' **(Skipper Jon Newsome on his winning goal against eventual Premiership champions Blackburn, 1994)**

'My game is all about finishing. The keeper came rushing out, I took it past him and once you get into those sorts of positions there's no need to rush. The calmer you are, the better the finish.' **(Jamie Cureton helps City beat Ipswich 3-0, March 1995)**

'There is always a fall guy in football and today that fell to me.' **(City goalkeeper Bryan Gunn kicks thin air at Portman Road and concedes a Robert Ullathorne own goal, 1996)**

'There are panels of three on a ball, so I line them up horizontally, going across the ball from top to bottom. I'll then try to hit the ball with the inside of my foot, across the panels, aiming the panels away from the goal and it curls the ball automatically.' **(Midfielder Ian Crook on the art of scoring from free kicks, 1996)**

'I certainly don't have a set celebration routine planned because it would go out of fashion before I scored a goal.' **(Skipper Matt Jackson scores the winner against Portsmouth, January 1997)**

'I can remember my dad coming from Swansea, one of the few times he had actually seen me play, and I scored really late on. And then I got sent off. There was a fracas in front of the dug-outs. I don't know what I was supposed to have done but the referee showed me a second yellow card and he never did tell me what it was for.' **(Chris Llewellyn scores City's last goal of the century against Queens Park Rangers, then gets a red card, December 1999)**

'It might look easy from the stand or when you're not the one taking it, but only people who take penalties know how difficult it is.' **(City winger Neil Adams, who failed only once from the spot)**

'This has always been a lucky ground for me. I scored two here as a kid for Watford, two for Leicester in a 4-2 defeat and now two today. I've actually played in Yorkshire derbies, East Midlands and West Midlands derbies and scored in all of them, but before today this is the only one I haven't scored in.' **(Iwan Roberts scores both goals in City's 2-0 win at Portman Road, March 2000)**

'We actually scored from Ipswich's corner. There weren't many seconds between Andy Marshall getting the ball and it finishing up in the Ipswich net.' **(Iwan Roberts on his second goal at Ipswich, March 2000)**

'I would like to add a few goals to my game. I think I got two or three in 200-odd games for Peterborough.' **(Adam Drury, 2001, who went on to score four times in 361 games for City)**

'I believe if a player is scoring goals and in form, you must keep playing him. I don't agree with all this squad rotation and resting players that we get today.' **(Ex-City striker Alan Taylor)**

'I thought it was a golden goal. There had been a couple of competitions in the years leading up to it where the golden goal had come into play and for some reason I thought that was going to carry on into this play-off final. I was heading towards the halfway line and Norwich fans thinking that I'd scored the goal that had taken us to the Premier League.' **(Iwan Roberts on his play-off final goal against Birmingham, 2002)**

'I didn't really know what to do. I just ran towards our fans and then all the lads jumped on top of me. But it would be nice to do it again at home.' **(Adam Drury scores his first City goal at Stoke, August 2002)**

'I'd love to be able to hang up my boots having scored 100 goals for Norwich. If I do that, I'd die a happy man.' **(Iwan Roberts, 2003, who was released on 96 goals a year later)**

'It was our first win at Coventry in a long, long time there. It was pleasing, especially as my brother went to the game as well. But he nipped to the toilet when I scored so he missed my goal. He came back up and everyone was celebrating and he got told I'd scored.' **(Gary Holt scores a rare goal, February 2004)**

'I went into a sort of Shefki Kuqi swan dive and then I had Iwan Roberts diving on my back, which is not the best thing.' **(Craig Fleming scores at Crewe, 2004)**

'I don't think I will ever forget this game for as long as I live.' **(Dean Ashton scores on his home debut, a 4-4 draw against Middlesbrough, 2005)**

'The fact that he was the Golden Boot winner from last season means nothing to me. He's paid to score goals, and he's scored them today. But he has also missed plenty lately. He's got another match ball to take home and put on his shelf, but that means more work for his wife with the dusting.' **(Glenn Roeder on Jamie Cureton's hat-trick against Colchester, March 2008)**

'I'm pretty lucky that I tend to score spectacular goals more than a lot of goals.' **(Darren Huckerby, 2008)**

'Goals were never a massive part of my game although I scored a few. I played on the left wing for most of my Norwich career and it would have been lovely to get to 50 goals but I was just short of it.' **(Darren Huckerby)**

'You just don't know when you hit it, whether it's going into the net or the back of the stand, but it's definitely up there as one of the best in my career.' **(Wes Hoolahan scores against Leicester, September 2010)**

'To tell you the truth I don't know what happened in the box for the winner. I just got lucky. It hit me in the midriff and it went in. When it went in it was a bit of a shock really. But I was just delighted that it helped us get the three points.' **(Simeon Jackson completes a hat-trick in a vital 3-2 home win over Derby, April 2011)**

'I said when I came on, at least I'm going to be playing in front of the Kop. To score in front of the Kop is a fantastic feeling.' **(Grant Holt scores the equaliser against Liverpool at Anfield on his 100th City appearance, 2011)**

'It's nice to score your first Premier League goal. It's a special one because it's my 100th career goal as well. To score it in the Premier League is just the way the script is written.' **(Aaron Wilbraham scores at Fulham, March 2012)**

'I'm not known for my heading but I'll take those all day. I knew Javier was going to whip the ball in so I just tried to get across my man and I got on the end of it and it went in the top corner.' **(Anthony Pilkington scores the winner against Manchester United, November 2012)**

'Yes I meant it – because I want to win the game. That's why I did it. I want to win every game. Would I do it again? If it was 0-0, yes. Ricky said put it in the back of the net, so I did. In Holland it's like that where if you get the throw-in you can play on.' **(City midfielder Leroy Foy defends his controversial disallowed goal against Cardiff, October 2013)**

'I don't know where that came from. But I've just seen Wayne Rooney has scored a goal at West Ham from the halfway line – so mine isn't even the goal of the day.' **(City midfielder Alex Tettey on his wonder goal against Sunderland, March 2014)**

(4)

Money, Money, Money

'What we are asking supporters to do is come to Carrow Road for better or worse, even if sometimes they see a bad game. It is on the money that comes through the turnstiles that we depend for our existence.' **(James Hanly, City chairman, 1956)**

'We criticise the recent addition of floodlighting because it could not be afforded.' **(City appeal committee report questions the £9,000 spent on lights, January 1957)**

'Although wages and salaries have been reduced the club will need a subsidy of £300 per week for the rest of the season. The present liabilities stand in excess of £20,000.' **(Appeal committee report, January 1957)**

'City are naturally anxious to qualify for the £750 winners' talent money and £25 per man final bonus. Who would not be?' **(David Dunn, *Pink Un*, looks ahead to the League Cup Final second leg against Rochdale, April 1962)**

'We both took a lot of stick when I signed him from Wrexham. Sandy Kennon was a favourite here and some people thought £6,500 was too much to spend on a goalkeeper.' **(Ron Ashman on signing Kevin Keelan, who went on to play 673 games)**

'When I met him at Carrow Road this week, Ron Davies struck me as a young man who is not going to be unduly bothered by a £35,000 tag.' **(Ted Bell, September 1963)**

'People talk about the money in the game but I wouldn't change anything about my life in football. I had some great times.' **(Centre-forward Laurie Sheffield)**

'I was on £32 10s a week at Norwich and when I went to Wolves they put me on £100, which was a lot of money at the time.' **(Hugh Curran recalls joining Wolves, 1969)**

'If I had a ha'penny for every single time I've seen that badge used I would be a millionaire by now. I got £10 and two directors' box tickets for a game.' **(Architect Andrew Anderson, who won the competition to design Norwich City's badge in 1971)**

'I think it is a sorry day when the club cannot afford to pay £8,000 for a Third Division footballer to try to help a manager in my predicament.' **(John Bond fails to sign Exeter's Lammie Robertson, August 1977)**

'I am not worried about the big price tag at the moment. This move must better my career. In any case, if Norwich did happen to go down, they would go straight back up.' **(Striker Phil Boyer signs for £145,000, February 1974)**

'An astroturf pitch is very expensive, it is true, but I wouldn't hesitate to spend £200,000 on one rather than buy another player for the same money.' **(John Bond's winter of discontent, January 1979)**

'I said to John Bond during the tour of Australia, where Fashanu was with the squad on such a trip for the first time, if I managed a club with £500,000 to spend there would be no better investment than this youngster.' **(Reserve team boss Mel Machin on Justin Fashanu, 1979)**

'We turned it down because we are going to build a team around him.' **(Chairman Sir Arthur South rejects £1m offer for striker Kevin Reeves, August 1979)**

'Don't do this too often, David, these cost 32 quid a time, you know.' **(Sir Arthur South presents Liverpool's David Fairclough with the match ball for his hat-trick, 1980)**

'The financial life of this club hangs on a very thin thread.' **(Financial director Ian Coutts, 1982 annual meeting)**

'Trying to walk the financial tightrope as we have been doing is frightening.' **(Sir Arthur South, 1982)**

'He was the easiest player I've had to deal with when he signed. There was no hustle, no outrageous demands for financial rewards. The whole thing was signed and sealed and completed in ten minutes.' **(Ken Brown on Mick Channon, December 1982)**

'I want no part of the present plans for the new Main Stand. By my reckoning this scheme could cost the club an extra £200,000 even though it appears cheaper initially.' **(Jimmy Jones resigns as a director, September 1985)**

'There is talk of a new TV deal being signed by the Premier League worth £50m and ten per cent of that is a lot of money. We aren't trying to rob anybody.' **(City goalkeeper and PFA representative Bryan Gunn, April 1992)**

'Personally I don't agree with a goal bonus. It can maybe make players selfish.' **(Striker Chris Sutton)**

'It comes down to me loudly and clearly that a wage bill of £3.8m for a staff of 35 players and eight coaching staff is enough. Everyone at some point is restricted by financial controls.' **(Chairman Robert Chase, November 1995)**

'The financial situation is still parlous, even with the loan from telecommunications giant A & T. Does this mean, incidentally, that the Clubcall line will now be charged at £10 a minute, with the club shop catalogue read out in full by a heavy stammerer before any information is given out?' **(Author and supporter Kevin Baldwin, 1996)**

'I was brought in in the last week of March and I realised within three days that the club was technically insolvent.' **(Chief executive Gordon Bennett, October 1996)**

'The new directors are likely to be producing quite a few rabbits out of their hats in the next two or three years which will greatly enhance the club's financial prospects.' **(Gordon Bennett, May 1997)**

'The patient is no longer in intensive care – now it's in the recovery ward.' **(Gordon Bennett on City's finances, 1998)**

'The ability of Norwich City to recruit big name players as they have in the past – Mick Channon, Martin O'Neill, Martin Peters – is a non-starter. One name I saw bandied about was Teddy Sheringham. His wages would have been £75,000 a month.' **(Gordon Bennett, 1999)**

'We've not got the money to be stupid. We are just poor millionaires.' **(Delia Smith, July 2000)**

'Coventry had been in the top flight for 34 years and one thing we couldn't legislate for was their relegation. It's disappointing but £5.3m is still a substantial amount and a record transfer for Norwich City.' **(Chairman Bob Cooper explains why the fee for Craig Bellamy was £1.2m lower than anticipated)**

'I'd be lying if I said I didn't think about the fee as it was a club record. It doesn't seem a lot of money now, but it was at the time. But I didn't have time to dwell on it.' **(Dean Ashton recalls his £3m move from Crewe)**

'Our planning for last season was a constant balancing act of prudence and ambition and we budgeted to finish last and for relegation.' **(Chief executive Neil Doncaster after relegation, 2005)**

'The big difference is the financial rewards in the game now. It's gone up tenfold in the last six or seven years. David Beckham earns as much in a week as we earned in a year.' **(Ex-City midfielder David Phillips)**

'I can get the same player in Scotland, sometimes better, for a quarter of the price you pay in England.' **(Manager Peter Grant, July 2007)**

'These players that I've been involved with, we were on two bob a week, it was nothing. These people are on £40,000 a week. It's not realistic for people who live their normal lives. That becomes a bit of a problem because it moves away from being just the normal working man's game. These people are millionaires.' **(Ted MacDougall, 2008)**

'I thought it may have been a bit higher, but at the end of the day, what we still have is 18,000-plus season ticket-holders showing their commitment, whether they're taking the rebate or not. The money goes straight to the manager's playing budget. You're talking about more than £700,000 in a League 1 budget.' **(Director Michael Foulger thanks fans who did not claim their relegation rebate, 2009)**

'Let's not forget where we were 12 months ago. The realism is that when the new board took control we had £23m of debt and an income plan which would not cover costs for the coming year, no way. We were heading for administration and we were in League 1. Our £23m of debt was weighing us down. Administration was a real possibility last autumn.' **(Chief executive David McNally, September 2010)**

'We have approached 52 potential investors around the world – in Europe, Russia, the Middle East, the Far East, the United States and, of course, the UK. We have had some expressions of interest. But every time when I asked the question, "Could you please verify you have funding?" no one passed the test.' **(Chairman Alan Bowkett, annual meeting, 2011)**

'We are now one of the few clubs in the Premier League making a profit – and one of the few clubs in the Premier League actually paying Corporation Tax, I suspect.' **(Alan Bowkett as City wipe out all external debt, October 2013)**

'The Premier League has been one of the most remarkable economic phenomena of the past 20 years and what goes with that is a set of activities and rules that you can't separate from it. If you are part of it, you have to get on with it.' **(Ex-City chairman Roger Munby)**

(5)

FA Cup

'They were all giants in all white with moustaches.'
**(Supporter G. Osborne describes City's FA Cup
conquerors Corinthians, 1929)**

'The omens were not good on a day that the City party
had to change buses between Liverpool Street station
and West London because of petrol and engine failure.'
**(*Eastern Evening News* report on 4-1 defeat at
Brentford, December 1931)**

'City were robbed at Portsmouth because Delapenha
knocked in the Pompey equaliser with his fist and I
thought Bill Lewis was going to tear the referee to pieces
in his righteous rage.' **(Peter Roberts on City's 1-1 FA
Cup third round draw at Portsmouth, 1950)**

'Came the replay and they were queueing from midnight
– queues back past Trowse station, way up Thorpe Road
and everywhere else and finally 43,129 got in. It was a
fantastic sight. There was no trouble, no mayhem, no
stabbings, missiles, assaults. My own recollection is there
was only one serious injury. A sailor fell off a tree which
used to overlook the Barclay Stand-South Bank corner
and broke his leg.' **(Peter Roberts on the FA Cup
replay against Portsmouth, 1950)**

'Norwich played football of a quality which we thought had deserted these islands. The Wembley Wizards, the present Spurs, the Moscow Dynamos, the fine England wartime teams – by any analysis, Norwich were as good as any.' **(Bob Ferrier on City's 3-1 FA Cup third round win over Liverpool, 1951)**

'The result wasn't a fluke. We were the better side. Ken Nethercott, Johnny Gavin, John Duffy and myself went to a pub off Northumberland Street and our celebrations were mushy peas and a pint. Football then was just a different world.' **(Two-goal Tom Docherty recalls the 3-1 win over Liverpool, 1951)**

'I don't remember it because of my own performance – I had so little to do. But it was a match which flowed all the time. There wasn't a single foul. I don't think the referee blew his whistle except for the kick-off and the end of the match.' **(Goalkeeper Ken Nethercott on beating Liverpool, 1951)**

'Arsenal were the champions so it was a great result. I think my clearest memory is that behind one of the Arsenal goals was this big clock and in the final 20 minutes, it just didn't seem to move. We were all looking at this clock and it seemed to fascinate us. We were watching the minutes tick by as we were trying to hang on.' **(Centre-half Reg Foulkes recalls the FA Cup shock win at Highbury, 1954)**

'The weather that day was very cold. I remember my father came down from Birmingham to watch the game and he was wearing his pyjamas under his suit.' **(Johnny Gavin on the win at Highbury, 1954)**

'They were two perfect centres. They were just asking to be hit – and I just hit them.' **(Tommy Johnston scores twice to beat Arsenal, 1954)**

'When we arrived at Thorpe Station we were greeted by what seemed like thousands of supporters. It was an incredible experience. I can still remember slipping away and going to the Lido with my girlfriend to celebrate.' **(Ron Hansell returns from the win at Arsenal, 1954)**

'It wasn't just that we had taken United to the cleaners and that one or two of them went missing on a frozen pitch. We had good players in our team, very good players who wouldn't have been out of their depth in the First Division. We weren't a kick-and-rush team and it just needed something to set it all off. Beating Manchester United did that for us.' **(Skipper Ron Ashman on City's 1959 FA Cup giant-killers)**

'I think what happened was that Archie Macaulay slowly got a side together and did what you should do. He started at the back and slowly worked to the front and I turned out to be the final cog. They had everything there except that the goals weren't going in. I went in and it all started to link together.' **(Centre-forward Terry Bly)**

'I was not too excited. Archie Macaulay had told me I was lucky to be retained by Norwich and that he was looking for another keeper so I just took each game as it came.' **(Goalkeeper Ken Nethercott on facing Manchester United in the FA Cup, 1959)**

'By your splendid achievements you have put Norwich on the map. On behalf of the citizens I wish you the best of luck and a very enjoyable game against Tottenham this afternoon.' **(Norman Tillett, Lord Mayor of Norwich, to manager Archie Macaulay, February 1959)**

'When I took up my position before kick-off in front of the crowd in the corner of the Barclay Stand and South Stand, the feeling was electric. It made my hair stand on end and I've never experienced anything like it.' **(Ron Ashman on the fifth round replay against Tottenham, 1959)**

'Cliff Jones, of Tottenham, reckoned I was the hardest full-back he ever played against. I don't know if he was right but you had to shake one or two of them up a bit.' **(Full-back Bryan Thurlow)**

'The Carrow Road replay was a game I was dreading. I had such mixed feelings after going straight from school to my local club, Norwich. I thought I had Terry Bly in my pocket that night but he got away once and that was the winning goal.' **(Tottenham centre-half Maurice Norman)**

'Bobby Smith had got up high and knocked the ball over the keeper's head. And Ken dived backwards and just managed to tip it over the bar – it was just magnificent. At that time I remember thinking, "What have I done?" I'd come to Norwich to play, and I couldn't see how I was going to get him out of the team.' **(Goalkeeper Sandy Kennon describes Ken Nethercott's wonder save against Tottenham, 1959)**

'Lots of players with bad injuries carried on playing in those days. That's what you did because teams didn't have substitutes. If you went off the field, you were letting the side down, so if at all possible you ignored the pain and got on with it. It was only for half an hour and I had nothing to do so it didn't matter.' **(Ken Nethercott dislocates his shoulder at Sheffield United, 1959)**

'The club, for me, will never repay Ken because if it hadn't have been for him, there wouldn't have been a replay and there wouldn't have been a next game. We didn't have substitutes and he stayed on the park.' **(Terry Bly pays tribute to Ken Nethercott)**

'Before the replay against Sheffield United, my wife and her father were reading the paper and saw the stories about whether it would be me or John Greatrex taking over in goal. There were pictures of us both. She said, "I hope Greatrex gets in because I don't like the look of that Kennon." Now we've been married for 25 years.' **(Sandy Kennon)**

'I'm glad it was Sandy out there, not me. He's a much better keeper than I am.' **(Ken Nethercott on the quarter-final replay against Sheffield United, 1959)**

'During the second half, when we were losing 1-0, I jumped with the goalkeeper [Ron Baynham] for a cross and he dropped the ball, and Errol Crossan knocked it into the net. But the referee disallowed the goal for a foul on the goalkeeper. Legally, you could challenge the goalkeeper in those days and I didn't foul him. I just jumped to head the ball and we collided.' **(Terry Allcock on City's disallowed goal in the semi-final against Luton, 1959)**

'We were playing badly – I don't know why. Everything was rushed down the right-hand side and I never kicked a ball in the first half. But I got a kick in the second half and got a goal.' **(Bobby Brennan scores against Luton, 1959)**

'It had to be the happiest birthday of my life at Tottenham when I scored. The fans were marvellous, and I felt I owed them something after their song for me at the start.' **(Bobby Brennan)**

'It was the biggest disappointment of my career. To play at Wembley was the ideal, the ambition of every professional footballer and I never did. I went there as a coach with Norwich and Manchester City in the League Cup, but it's not the same as playing. The previous season I had played in a couple of rounds of the FA Cup for Bolton and scored in them, before I joined Norwich. Bolton went on to beat Manchester United in the final, so in a sense I missed out two years in a row.' **(Terry Allcock on the semi-final replay defeat by Luton)**

'I reckon we had about 80 per cent of the play in the replay and just couldn't score. There was even one occasion when McNally, the Luton right-back, was running across the goal line and Jimmy Hill's shot hit the top of his boot and ballooned over the bar. If we had played for four hours, I don't think we would have scored.' **(Bryan Thurlow)**

'I saw grown men cry, I saw big, strong men cry. I cried myself.' **(Sandy Kennon on the semi-final replay defeat by Luton, 1959)**

'I've never seen so many grown men crying or near to crying. There were even tears in the bath. It hurt so much because we felt Luton were there for the taking. They had given us less trouble than almost anyone. We had come all that way just to be beaten like that.' **(Ron Ashman)**

'Everyone was very, very flat. Anyone who has lost in a semi-final will know it just leaves you speechless. You don't converse. I don't know if there were tears. I was too busy stomping about.' **(Bobby Brennan)**

'It was the conclusion of an excellent week for me because I had scored my 100th goal for the club when we beat Stoke 6-0 the previous Saturday, then scored four when we beat Newcastle 5-0 in the FA Cup fourth round game in midweek. Then getting two goals at Manchester City in the fifth round capped a fine week.' **(Terry Allcock goes goal crazy, March 1963)**

'We had five FA Cup games all crammed into less than a month. We had beaten Newcastle 5-0 in the fourth round, which was the game where I was spotted and which led to my move. We had great expectations and we thought we could beat Leicester at home in the quarter-final but we lost 2-0 and Terry Allcock missed a penalty. We had gone through the rounds very quickly but it all came to a very abrupt end.' **(Ollie Burton on City's FA Cup exit, 1963)**

'I had broken a metatarsal and at midday on the morning of the Leicester game I went to the Norfolk & Norwich Hospital for an injection. But after about an hour it had worn off and it was killing me. Then, to cap it all, I missed a penalty.' **(Terry Allcock)**

'Tommy Bryceland crossed the ball in from the left wing and United came out expecting the offside flag. In fact the first thing I did was look across to the linesman before running on. Then I saw Alex Stepney coming out and just pushed it past him. It made me feel ten feet tall.' **(Don Heath scores in City's 2-1 FA Cup fourth round win at Manchester United, 1967)**

'I got a kick in the mouth from David Sadler which left me with a split lip. I had to run around carrying this piece of cotton wool for the rest of the game.' **(No running repairs for goalscorer Don Heath at Old Trafford)**

'We were taking a battering but their back four got possession and I was running around like an idiot. Then Tony Dunne played a backpass towards Alex Stepney in goal, but he had come out and it flew past him. I was racing in and I caught it about two yards from the line. It was going in but I knocked it in anyway.' **(Gordon Bolland recalls his winning goal at Manchester United, 1967)**

'It was the Great Train Robbery all over again. We had made brave noises in the dressing room before the match but we did not give ourselves much of a chance in all honesty. Even afterwards it took a long while for it to sink in that we had done it.' **(Kevin Keelan on City's win at Old Trafford, 1967)**

'We tried to ruffle them straightaway to knock their confidence, and Nobby Stiles met his match with Tommy Bryceland, who was a much better player than most people gave him credit for.' **(Mal Lucas)**

'We beat them more easily than the 2-1 scoreline suggests. Dave Stringer crunched into George Best right at the start and I knew then he wouldn't want to know for the rest of the game. He didn't.' **(Centre-half Laurie Brown)**

'The board couldn't understand why I wasn't going to watch United play beforehand. I had to explain that there wasn't much anyone didn't know about a team that boasted the likes of Best, Charlton, Law and Stiles.' **(Manager Lol Morgan forgoes a spying mission on Manchester United, 1967)**

'The best silverware was brought out. And we had our pot of tea. The lasting impression was that they thought we were in for a hiding but they wanted to make the day special for us. As far as they were concerned, we were like lambs being led to the slaughter and they were going to make it a day to remember for us.' **(Lol Morgan is invited for pre-match tea by Manchester United boss Matt Busby, 1967)**

'The result, achieved by a side struggling in mid-table Division Two and deprived of their two leading scorers, must rank as one of the most astonishing one-off performances in the club's history. They were magnificent.' **(Bruce Robinson, *Eastern Daily Press*, on the FA Cup win at Old Trafford, 1967)**

'By this time I was getting towards the end of my career.
I'd broken both legs and I was feeling it. The only way we
survived was because of our aerial strength. I like to think
I was a constructive player, but in games like that those
thoughts all go by the board. It was just a question of
winning the ball and clearing it.' **(Terry Allcock on the
win at Old Trafford, 1967)**

'Poor old Matt looked very pale, very drawn and was
moist around the eyes, but he came in nevertheless,
shook hands with people, congratulated them and then
wandered off. He left the impression of being a very great
gentleman.' **(Bruce Robinson, *Eastern Daily Press*
reporter, on Matt Busby's reaction to City's FA Cup
win, 1967)**

'It's a big let-down. Just as we get something going,
along comes this business to upset our rhythm and
cause fixture congestion. We're victims of a club with
inadequate resources.' **(John Bond laments a fifth
round postponement caused by Bradford City's flu
outbreak, February 1976)**

'I want to congratulate Bradford. They came to do
a job and they did it well but of course I'm bitterly
disappointed.' **(John Bond on City's shock 2-1 FA
Cup home defeat by Bradford City, February 1976)**

'I remember it very well and I remember the headline
"Kitchen sinks Norwich".' **(Phil Hoadley recalls
helping Orient to a shock third round win at
Carrow Road, 1978)**

'I tried to come back too soon. John Bond asked me to
play in the FA Cup at Leicester. It was on a bone-hard
pitch, I was only 75 per cent fit and I was terrible and
should have been taken off. I tried to do my best, but
then John slated me for my performance and said it was

the worst he had seen from a centre-forward.' **(Martin Chivers on the 3-0 defeat at Filbert Street, 1979)**

'I have some pleasant memories of games against Norwich, including the infamous white tights episode in the FA Cup.' **(Former Leicester winger Keith Weller)**

'People still remember it because it was Goal of the Season. I have a lovely platter to remind me and I can watch it on YouTube as well. Ally Robertson lobbed the ball up to me and I chested it down and turned away from Martin O'Neill and Steve Walford, and I had a go and it flew past Chris Woods to his left.' **(West Bromwich Albion's Cyrille Regis ends City's FA Cup hopes, 1982)**

'The FA Cup just seems to draw something out of Norfolk folk. I don't honestly know exactly why but the city of Norwich is a different place when the Canaries are involved in cup football. There is an unseen feeling of excitement about the people and the place.' **(Manager Ken Brown, 1983)**

'My best local derby memory of all was scoring that winning goal, and the worst was getting kicked all around the pitch by Osman and Butcher in return.' **(Keith Bertschin recalls his fifth round goal against Ipswich, 1983)**

'We were conned, conned by an old pro who knows all the tricks of the trade.' **(Ken Brown laments Jimmy Case's controversial winner for Brighton in the quarter-final, 1983)**

'Enough, no more; 'tis not so sweet now as it was before.' **(Chairman Robert Chase quotes Shakespeare for the benefit of poetry lover and Sutton United boss Barrie Williams after their 8-0 fourth round defeat, 1989)**

'I was stranded near the penalty spot and could only watch hopelessly over my shoulder as Pat Nevin got the slightest of touches and the ball trickled over the line and into the net. It seemed to take an eternity; my momentum was still carrying me forward and it was a horrible goal to see going in, as if in slow-motion. It was a poxy goal to concede.' **(Bryan Gunn on City's semi-final defeat by Everton, 1989)**

'We were devastated to have lost our semi-final but when we stopped off at Newport Pagnell on the way home for a bite to eat and saw the TV screens with the news coming through, I remember being with Trevor Putney and there were tears in our eyes. It was horrendous. It's not easy to speak about it, even now.' **(Bryan Gunn recalls news of Hillsborough, 1989)**

'The crowd knew it before we did. We were hearing reports coming through from the other semi-final because Liverpool were in it. There are Everton and Liverpool supporters in the same family and they were worried. Even the players had people who were at the game as well, so the Everton players were worried to think some of their relatives had been involved. That put a big dampener on the day for them in terms of winning and going to the final. Our result didn't seem to matter as much when you heard what had happened.' **(Manager Dave Stringer on City's defeat in the 'other' semi-final, 1989)**

'In the circumstances our semi-final was just completely forgotten about afterwards. I don't know if I've ever even seen the goal on television.' **(Bryan Gunn remembers Villa Park and Hillsborough semi-finals, 1989)**

'Just one more thing. I hope Norwich City go on to win the FA Cup.' **(Manchester United boss Alex Ferguson after a fifth round exit at the hands of Norwich, February 1991)**

'All I aimed to do was get it on target. Some will say it was lucky, but I thought I meant to do what I did. It did seem to take an age to loop over the top of Tim Flowers and go in, though.' **(Chris Sutton scores a quarter-final replay winner against Southampton, 1992)**

'I think my players are competitive. I think they work hard and the rest is up to the referee. If the referee sees fit to caution players or send them off that's up to him.' **(Southampton manager Ian Branfoot after his team finished their quarter-final replay at Norwich with nine men, 1992)**

'One minute it was Stringer out and now we're on the march with Stringer's army.' **(Dave Stringer prepares for the 1992 semi-final)**

'It wasn't the greatest day. I remember we stopped on the way home at Saracen's Head on the A17 and someone had put on a spread, but there were tears shed after that game and that was the first time I'd seen that.' **(City defender Colin Woodthorpe on the 1992 semi-final defeat by Sunderland)**

'As the hapless Simon Tracey, on loan but not for long, finally collected a ball cleanly the chant hurled back at him was a bitterly ironic "England's Number One".' **(Graham Dunbar on City's 5-0 defeat at Everton, 1995)**

'It's like a period of mourning. I'm hurt and the players are very hurt.' **(John Deehan on the 5-0 defeat at Everton, 1995)**

'If I didn't feel the changes could have got us the win I would not have made those changes, and I had a team out there that was good enough to win this football match. As manager of this football club, I will always take responsibility. It's an awful day for us.' **(Manager Chris Hughton defends making six changes as City suffer a shock fourth round exit at home to non-league Luton, 2013)**

(6)

Refs, Rants And Rows

'I remember my debut because I gave away a penalty against Crystal Palace. I still remember the referee. It was Ray Tinkler from Boston and I sometimes see him on my travels. It was a very harsh award, I thought.' **(Duncan Forbes concedes a spot-kick, but Palace miss it, October 1968)**

'The fee a referee now receives is ten guineas. When I was on the [Football] League list the fee was three guineas, the meal and hotel allowance was much smaller and we travelled second-class.' **(City secretary and former referee Bert Westwood, 1970)**

'Bad refereeing just promotes trouble.' **(Kevin Keelan, 1978)**

'I did not see the incident. Photographers have been known to be biased and Charlie thought he was going to keep the ball. This man has assured us he was an impartial member of the Press and he had no intention of doing so. But Charlie has said he was sorry and as far as I'm concerned that's the end of the matter. Now why don't you write about football?' **(Southampton manager Lawrie McMenemy defends Charlie**

George after he struck photographer Jack Spencer at Carrow Road, 1980)

'In my view there was some provocation but standards have to be maintained.' **(Southampton manager Lawrie McMenemy performs a U-turn as he suspends Charlie George for a week and fines him a week's wages)**

'If I had thought it was a deliberate assault I would have dismissed the player and may well have pressed charges, too.' **(Referee David Axcell is in forgiving mood after being flattened by Charlton full-back Mark Reid at Carrow Road, January 1987)**

'It was very difficult. I had to keep the players away from the politics of what was going on outside and try to concentrate on what we were doing.' **(Manager Dave Stringer amid boardroom upheaval, 1988)**

'I don't think I've ever walked away from a football ground feeling as hard done by as I did on Saturday.' **(Dave Stringer on the controversial 4-3 defeat at Arsenal, November 1989)**

'I don't think he's in the right frame of mind at the moment. Some players go through this and coming out of the side will perhaps shake him out of that mood and revitalise his appetite for play.' **(Dave Stringer drops striker Robert Rosario for what proved to be the last time, January 1991)**

'I honestly believe I should be in the side but it looks like the cleaner has a better chance of getting in than me at the moment.' **(Tim Sherwood, October 1991)**

'He has made me a scapegoat to take the spotlight from his own failings. I don't think I can play for the manager again unless he apologises. I went out of my way to protect the boss and take the pressure off him and this is the thanks I get for it.' **(Mark Bowen, dropped by Dave Stringer, February 1992)**

'Mark has looked a little bit tired at times and there have been a few other players who have been tired, too. But he's a good player and a good captain and I'm sure he'll be back in the future – if Colin Woodthorpe lets him.' **(Dave Stringer on Mark Bowen, February 1992)**

'There was a bit of a fracas and once I cooled that down, I consulted the linesman. I had no choice but to backtrack.' **(Referee Kevin Lynch changes his mind over an Ipswich penalty award at Norwich, November 1995)**

'He waited a good minute after giving the spot-kick to rule it out. Nobody knows who was offside. It must have been the Invisible Man.' **(Ipswich manager George Burley criticises referee Kevin Lynch, November 1995)**

'I would still like Dean Windass at this club and I would like him before the end of the century.' **(Manager Martin O'Neill voices his frustration over attempts to sign the Hull forward, 1995)**

'I know it was me that started this off by deciding to come back here, but there was no malice intended in what was done. I think there has been malice in what was written.' **(Ian Crook on his U-turn over joining Ipswich, 1996)**

'It's not often you find a referee that both sides can't stand the sight of.' **(Ian Crook, September 1996, after 1-0 win over Wolves)**

'The referee could have sent off 14 and abandoned the match.' **(Crystal Palace manager Dave Bassett, 1996, after a 21-man brawl against City)**

'Something has got to be done because we can't go on like this. It's absolutely ridiculous.' **(Manager Mike Walker on referee Andy D'Urso's four red cards and nine yellows in a 2-0 home win over Huddersfield, March 1997)**

'I want to apologise to all the Reading players and fans. It's never happened to me before in 31 years of refereeing. You don't know how bad I feel.' **(Neale Barry on his unlikely assist for Phil Mulryne's winning goal, April 2004)**

'The assistant has flagged and there is a buzzer in his flag but as he has buzzed the flag has slipped out of his hand. At that stage nobody could say it was a clear goalscoring opportunity. So play has gone on and there has been another foul, which was a clear goalscoring opportunity. We have penalised the first opportunity.' **(Referee Graham Poll fails to give Arsenal defender Lauren a red card for hauling down Darren Huckerby, August 2004)**

'Fifteen bloody minutes to go, we're 1-0 up and we want to win the game, we need a little bit of help. They got that grit and they got that passion, but the players never got anything back in return. Not for 94 minutes did they get anything and for me that's a disgrace.' **(City boss Peter Grant criticises the fans after a 1-1 draw against Hull, November 2006)**

'What I don't like is the way people in and around the club have tried to say there is a problem between the two of us. He has gone out of his way to say there isn't. I have gone out of my way – although I don't feel I have to go out of my way – to say there isn't. And yet these nasty, irritating people that try to cause confrontation between myself and a player, between myself and supporters, are just bad people.' **(Glenn Roeder denies a rift with Darren Huckerby, February 2008)**

'We played fantastic and because one man can't get a Sunday morning refereeing decision correct, we get beaten. And if I never see Andy D'Urso again, I'll be the happiest man in the world.' **(Glenn Roeder, March 2008)**

'It would have been ideal to come back here but that wasn't to be. I would have loved to have come back to the club but the manager at the time, for one reason or another, didn't want to take me so that was that, really.' **(Chris Sutton is denied a second spell with City)**

'I thought Andy D'Urso was a mate of mine because he ran the line in my testimonial match and I gave him a DVD player. I went in to see Andy and I think he knows he made a mistake. You can look in people's eyes and you can know that. He didn't say anything, I didn't get anything from him at all. Andy has a DVD of the game – I hope it's still working.' **(Manager Bryan Gunn on a disputed penalty and red card for Gary Doherty against Bristol City, February 2009)**

'I never said a word. All I did was kick the ball back, to keep the ball in play. He just said, "You're off." I've done it a million times this season – get on the pitch and kick the ball back to keep the game flowing. I just thought that game was too big for that referee. I think with the cameras on him, he wanted to be the main point of attention.' **(Manager Paul Lambert, sent to the stands at Tranmere, April 2010)**

'He can go away, the referee, and go and do his job, in the kindergarten or somewhere where he works. If he works there, he probably gets that wrong as well.' **(Paul Lambert after a 3-3 draw at Reading, November 2010)**

'It's been ridiculous, it really has. It's escalated into something that was going out of control. The media don't help, not every one of you, but some of you just fuel it – add two and two and come up with about 949, which was wrong. You were telling people that I was leaving and I don't hang about clubs for that long. That's lies, that's not right. I was never going to walk out with the rapport I've got with the fans here.' **(Paul Lambert reacts to being linked with Burnley, January 2011)**

(7)

Ron Manager

'Ron Saunders arrived at Carrow Road at about the time men first landed on the moon, but he was a man with his feet firmly on the ground.' **(Bruce Robinson, *Passing Seasons*)**

'Saunders was a hard disciplinarian and everything was geared to defending and stopping the other team, whereas Bondy wasn't very interested in tackling and defending.' **(Full-back Geoff Butler)**

'I can only thank Ron Saunders for taking me from Coventry. I didn't even know where Norwich was but I signed that same night.' **(Midfielder Graham Paddon)**

'If a player is not of a strong character, and of the right type, then no matter how much ability he has he will never be in the top bracket. It is essential that the people you bring into your club are equivalent to the type of person you would take home to meet your own family.' **(Ron Saunders, 1970)**

'Training was very intensive. Our fitness levels under Ron Saunders meant we were better prepared than anyone else in the division, and put that together with some good footballers and you can see why we were successful.' **(Midfielder Doug Livermore recalls promotion to the First Division, 1972)**

'In a terrible snowstorm at Birmingham last Saturday we received our biggest defeat of the season when we went down 4-0. To listen to some people talking, this defeat is a tragedy. This of course is a load of rubbish.' **(Ron Saunders, March 1972)**

'When you consider the strength of Birmingham that season, with Trevor Francis, Bob Latchford and Bob Hatton scoring all those goals, it was great what we did.' **(Jim Bone on promotion to the First Division, 1972)**

'I think we were a little bit nervous and at first the priority was not to lose but fortunately I stuck one in and we took advantage and once we were two up it more or less sealed it. It wasn't a great game.' **(Ken Foggo on City's promotion-clinching 2-1 win at Orient, 1972)**

'I told my grandchildren I rose high enough to see the Watford town hall clock and headed it past the keeper and several people on the line.' **(Dave Stringer recalls his Second Division title-winning goal at Watford, 1972)**

'First Division football has always been the club's ultimate objective. There have been dark times when it has seemed as far away as, until recent years, was space travel to the moon.' **(City chairman Geoffrey Watling hails promotion, April 1972)**

'The number one job of any manager is to get 11 men in every team giving him not 100 but 101 per cent.' **(Ron Saunders, 1972)**

'I came in at the start of the Ron Saunders reign, and saw him transform an average Division Two outfit into a First Division force. I can make no comparisons with previous Carrow Road managers, but it is unlikely that any of his predecessors ruled with so obvious an iron fist.' **(Keith Skipper, *Eastern Daily Press*, 1972)**

'We were unfashionable. We were one of the first teams that got the midfield and defence to push out to halfway. We didn't mean to play offside but the back four got out very quickly. A lot of the purists didn't like that but we played good football as well.' **(Graham Paddon)**

'I had a feeling that Saunders was thinking about a four-man midfield without me. I felt I could have played in a deeper role but it was not to be. I was extremely disappointed that he never actually told me face to face.' **(Ken Foggo)**

'This week, even 40 years on, I had a fan come up to me in the street and say, "You're Max Briggs," and start to talk about the team.' **(Ex-City midfielder Max Briggs, 2012)**

'When I first did the job I knew little about Norwich but I learned quite a lot. I didn't know the players but Ron Saunders invited me to Hull for a League Cup tie to see the game, stay in the hotel and chat to the players. Ron wouldn't give any secrets away but people like him and Duncan Forbes and Dave Stringer carried the club forward. It was all less sophisticated then, but you could speak to the players. You didn't have to be bosom pals but they were more accessible.' **(*Match of the Week* commentator Gerry Harrison)**

'Make no mistake about it, it's very tough penetrating Norwich's 4-4-2 defensive set-up but it's almost impossible to overcome the last barrier in the shape of Keelan – a miracle-worker.' **(Chelsea assistant manager Ron Suart, 1972)**

'I don't think we took our eye off the ball because of the League Cup but in the end it was too much for us. I was physically tired from the games. It took its toll on a tired team but we signed Colin Suggett, Trevor Hockey and

Ian Mellor and it made that little bit of difference and we stayed up.' **(Striker David Cross)**

'Let's face it, we've had a fright to go with all the glory but I'm now convinced we wouldn't get into this sort of predicament again.' **(Kevin Keelan on City's narrow escape from relegation, 1973)**

'When I came to Norwich, Ron Saunders sat me down and explained his rules and I said straightaway, "I won't have a problem because they're exactly the same rules as Bill Shankly's."' **(Doug Livermore)**

'Ron Saunders would have you running up and down hills. We used to have a full day's training every Thursday and my legs were gone for Saturday. I always say I lost at least a yard of pace while I was at Norwich because of that.' **(Ian Mellor)**

'It's a good thing when fans really identify with a player, particularly in a club like ours. It helps my game.' **(Graham Paddon, 1973)**

'The way Ron played made it difficult to score too many goals. He tended to play just one of us up front. Ron's attitude was that we started with a point, we weren't going to concede goals and anything we got on top of that was a bonus.' **(Striker Peter Silvester)**

'Ron Saunders got the best out of the players at his disposal and without what he achieved, would John Bond have come to Norwich and would the club have gone on to success under Ken Brown, Dave Stringer and Mike Walker?' **(Full-back Clive Payne)**

'I didn't work for Norwich City. I worked for Geoffrey Watling. We had a wonderful working relationship. He was everything a manager could want in a chairman. It was a shock to us all when he stepped down from the chair and a few months after that I packed up and left. He was a one-off. He was completely special, not just as a chairman but as a person.' **(Ron Saunders's tribute on the death of Geoffrey Watling, November 2004)**

(8)

Fans For All Seasons

'I am delighted that Norwich have today become champions of the Second Division. Please convey my warmest congratulations to their manager and to all members of the team and my best wishes for next season in the First Division – Elizabeth R Queen Mother.' **(Telegram to Lord Mayor of Norwich, April 30, 1972)**

'The crowd seemed to cling like a swarm of bees to the face of the cliff.' **(Eric Fowler describes The Nest)**

'Behind me on the terraces was a hefty Norfolk lass who, as the ball entered the net, raised her arms with a shout of "goal" and brought both fists down on my head with a crash. When I recovered I found the goal disallowed. It is still a sore point – the goal and not my head.' **(Lord Wallace of Coslany recalls the 1959 FA Cup semi-final against Luton)**

'It was the biggest disappointment in all my time supporting City – to get so close. My diary entry the next day says, "Still depressed." And I've written that all the papers said we should have won.' **(Myra Hawtree on the 1959 FA Cup semi-final replay defeat by Luton)**

'The attitude of the crowd means a lot to a player. He knows that if he scores a goal he will be cheered to the echo, but if he has a bad game the fans will not be slow to let him know about it. He's got to accept that as part and parcel of the game.' **(Archie Macaulay, October 1961)**

'When I take the field at Carrow Road, my thoughts are for the 16,000 hardcore supporters.' **(Defender Laurie Brown, 1967)**

'At Norwich you were a hero. You would go into shops and be recognised, anything you bought you got for half the price. If you wanted to buy a car they'd take a few hundred quid off it. If you wanted tyres on your car, they couldn't do enough for you.' **(Striker Hugh Curran)**

'We have been most impressed by the exemplary behaviour of the Norwich City supporters whilst travelling to away matches by British Rail and would very much like to express our appreciation by donating the ball for the home match with Blackpool on 25th March.' **(British Rail letter, March 1972)**

'A yellow and green trail snaked all the way from East Anglia to London and back.' **(Ted Bell recalls City's promotion night at Orient, 1972)**

'I played against them early this season and recall getting some stick from the crowd. I love it really, although I must point out that I don't take kindly to stick from the home fans.' **(Trevor Hockey signs from Sheffield United, February 1973)**

'Graham Paddon is the idol of every schoolboy in Norfolk, elegant, fair-haired, bearded, driving on with his hair streaming back like a young Viking, to plunder the Arsenal goal three times in his great hat-trick in

November against my old club at Highbury.' **(Rt Rev Maurice Wood, Bishop of Norwich, 1973)**

'No Reeves, No Future, No Fans' **(Supporters' banner at Kevin Reeves's final game, 1980)**

'When you're playing you don't realise how much the football club means to the public. When you travel with the fans you can tell how big a part of their lives it is. You get to know them and realise how much it means to them.' **(Duncan Forbes, Club Canary travel boss, 1981–88)**

'I shall ask the police to turn away anyone going to that end of the ground if they are wearing scarves, have shaven heads or are wearing bovver boots. It is up to us to prevent these louts from getting into the game. If it's a fight they want, that's what they will get.' **(City chairman Sir Arthur South reacts to referee Brian Hill being struck by a cigarette lighter thrown from the Barclay Stand, March 1982)**

'I was more concerned with beating Ipswich than getting to Wembley. What capped it all was seeing Terry Butcher come past wiping tears from his eyes.' **(David Hewison enjoys the Milk Cup semi-final victory, 1985)**

'At a time when soccer is pilloried by its enemies and sickened by the mindless violence of louts, these two teams and their supporters put the pride and sanity back into our national game.' **(Martin Hardy on the Milk Cup Final, 1985)**

'This was the friendliest final for years. We were delighted with the fans' behaviour. It has restored my faith in football.' **(Police Commander David Polkinghorne, Wembley, 1985)**

'I used to think a ban on away fans was the answer to football hooliganism but now I believe all it does is push the problem to one side.' **(Ken Brown, October 1986)**

'They used to boo when my name was read out. It was really, really difficult. You have to stand up and fight because it can make or break a player. I'd like to think it made me stronger. The turning point was when I scored my first goal in a 2-0 win at Leicester. The first time they cheered my name I stood in front of the dug-out and bowed to all four corners of the ground.' **(Ex-Ipswich star Trevor Putney finally wins over City fans)**

'Following City is a way of life for me. It's a bit like a drug that I am addicted to and I don't really think of not going.' **(Angus George, who watched 1,186 consecutive games home and away from 1978 to 2001)**

'I got the ferry from Harwich to Gothenburg. I spent 23 hours on the ferry then drove from Gothenburg to Stockholm on the Saturday, managed to find the ground on the Sunday, and it turned out I was the only Norwich fan there. I was really disappointed.' **(Richard Bland travels to a pre-season friendly in Sweden, 1993)**

'This has been the best day of my life – really tremendous.' **(Supporter Derek Bill after watching City play in Milan, 1993)**

'The club seemed small-minded at times but not the public of Norwich. They were the most complete football-minded people I ever came across. It was the only place I know where you could walk down the street and everybody would know you.' **(Laurie Brown, 1994)**

'We are hopeful that the club will become nearer to the supporters now the former chairman has left.' **(Roy**

Blower, chairman of Norwich City Independent Supporters' Association, on the exit of Robert Chase, 1996)

'I'd always wanted to score at Carrow Road so I could celebrate in front of the fans. But I scored at the opposite end to where the Norwich fans were at Maine Road and the main thing I remember was just how quiet the place went. You could have heard a pin drop.' **(Adrian Coote clinches City's first win at Manchester City for 33 years, 1997)**

'I have always wanted to sit in the Barclay End and sing "Adrian Forbes, my Lord" to the tune of "Kumbaya".' **(Delia Smith, 1997)**

'It's pretty hard to put into words. I thought we'd just walk on there and walk off again. But we went round and there were actually guys bowing at us. It was unbelievable.' **(Canadian winger Errol Crossan at the 1959 reunion at Carrow Road, 1999)**

'Most treasured Norwich City souvenir? Mike, my husband, as I found him at a Norwich away game.' **(City fan Judy Trivett)**

'My favourites are my Norwich City FC knickers.' **(Pop star Sophie Ellis-Bextor, 2000)**

'It was very emotional but through all that emotion football is football. That's how it is. It's joy and it's extreme suffering.' **(Delia Smith on City's play-off final defeat, 2002)**

'A few people booed when I first said I wanted to look round, but after that everywhere I went people were wanting me to stay.' **(Midfielder Phil Mulryne eventually signs a new contract, 2002)**

'A football club is only as good as its supporters. We're lucky to have the best fans in the world.' **(Delia Smith, 2004)**

'A message for the best football supporters in the world. We need a 12th man here. Where are you? Where are you? Let's be 'avin you. Come on!' **(Delia Smith's famous speech on pitch at half-time, February 2005)**

'I was shocked at just how good the supporters at Fulham were. They were fantastic, really fantastic. For them to give us that kind of reception after that performance, having watched us lose 6-0, I'd never seen anything like that before.' **(City striker Dean Ashton, 2005)**

'During my time at Norwich I can honestly say that was my most favourite spell in my ten years in England. The supporters were with us in the good times when we won the Championship but they were also there in the worst times like when we got relegated from the Premier League.' **(Swedish striker Mathias Svensson)**

'Yvette realises there are certain games that you have to go to.' **(Ed Balls, politician and City fan, has a sympathetic wife)**

'I don't know why they chose me. I only went to 13 of the away games last season.' **(City fan Maurice Sills, 92, is named 2007 Supporter of the Year by the Association of Provincial Football Supporters' Clubs in London)**

'My first game, the atmosphere inside Carrow Road, I didn't realise it could get as serious as that.' **(Glenn Roeder, 2007)**

'I wasn't very familiar with the team at the time but the yellow and green caught my eyes instantly because it reminded me of the lovebirds I kept when I was seven.' **(Hong Kong-based City fan, David Lee)**

'Ron Davies is without doubt the greatest striker ever to play for Norwich City and if he was not selected it would be a grave injustice.' **(George Lovett on the Greatest Ever debate, 2008)**

'I am as frustrated as any supporter. I sometimes wonder if all of them understand that I am as frustrated as all of them. I want to win. It's our life. Football becomes like a drug if you've been in it all your life. You need the fix.' **(Glenn Roeder, January 2009)**

'There were almost 3,000 fans who had travelled down to London and they deserve much better than what they have been getting over the last two or three weeks.' **(Loan striker Arturo Lupoli's goal at Charlton earns an FA Cup replay, 2009)**

'It's horrible playing in front of 3,000 supporters when you're 3-0 down after 30 minutes. I can hear everything that's going on and I'm not going to be stupid and say anything less.' **(Goalkeeper David Marshall after a 4-2 defeat at Charlton means relegation, May 2009)**

'The great thing about supporting a club like Norwich is that the pain of losing is not as intense as the joy of winning. It's a matter of expectation.' **(Stephen Fry, 2009)**

'All the papers were giving Gary Doherty rubbish but he's one of my favourite players. He's a bit like Marmite, people either love him or hate him but I'm one of those people who thinks he's brilliant.' **(Harry Dawson, lead singer and guitarist, We Can't Dance)**

'God bless those people over there. When I was there they were incredible, the best fans you could have behind you, a fantastic bunch of people.' **(Kevin Keelan, 2010)**

'I know how vital it is to Norwich fans to try to win it. I think any derby you play in, whether you're in Madrid or Germany or Norwich, any derby you want to look at, there is the same passion. I know in no uncertain terms how important it is to the people of Norwich to try to win that game.' **(Paul Lambert looks forward to welcoming Ipswich, 2010)**

'We are a bit sad about it but nothing stays the same forever. It has been an absolute delight to be able to serve the club the way we have.' **(John Landamore, chairman of Friends of Norwich City Youth, brings down the curtain after raising £363,696 in 16 years)**

'He got the name wrong. He doesn't mean Norwich City, he means Premiership Norwich City, which is more than you can say for any football team in Suffolk.' **(Shadow Chancellor Ed Balls replies to West Suffolk MP Matthew Hancock, 2012)**

'To be voted for by the fans is a great honour. You always try to give your best and to get this sort of praise it just makes you want to give them something back and try to be the best you can.' **(Sebastien Bassong becomes the first overseas winner of the City player of the year award, 2013)**

'I love all sports. I'm a Norwich City football fan, no one is upset with you for supporting Norwich.' **(Hugh Jackman, 2015)**

(9)

Game for a Laugh

'People didn't realise I couldn't see under those old floodlights. The club got me some contact lenses. It cost them £100 and they sent someone from London to test me. But I never wore them once. I couldn't put them in. Archie Macaulay would ask, "Have you got them in?" and I'd say yes, but I never did.' **(City half-back Matt Crowe)**

'If you fail the medical we'll sack the doctor.' **(Chairman Geoffrey Watling to new signing Ron Davies, September 1963)**

'We called him the beefy full-back from Fray Bentos. If the opposing winger was likely to be timid, Ron Saunders would probably play Blackie. He was an excellent professional. He was also undoubtedly the comedian of the team. He was my next door neighbour and I soon discovered he was not the man to ask for DIY advice when he drilled a hole through his bedroom wall – into mine.' **(Duncan Forbes fondly remembers Alan Black)**

'I named Dave in my Norwich City Dream Team. He was very strong to play alongside and very difficult to beat, so much so they always called us "tight at the back". In fact, Dave was arrested last week for breaking into a £10

81

note, but they let him off because it was his first offence.'
(Duncan Forbes on Dave Stringer)

'York City, the team who wear their Y-fronts on top of their shorts.' **(Gerry Harrison, *Match of the Week* commentator, Norwich v York, 1975)**

'I am not saying he's tight but he's the only guy I know who turns the gas off to turn the bacon over.' **(Ted MacDougall on Duncan Forbes)**

'The City and Birmingham players were heading for the dressing room when Mr Salmon was reminded that most games span an hour and a half, not counting the interval. He covered his embarrassment with a drop ball.' **(Keith Skipper on referee Ken Salmon, who blew up too early at Carrow Road, September 1976)**

'I don't think we got Muzinic. I reckon they sent his milkman.' **(Striker Justin Fashanu has doubts about City's record signing, 1981)**

'At the time of the second goal they actually had a fan on the pitch. We called him the Milk Tray man because he was dressed all in black, if you remember the advert. If Gary Bannister hadn't headed it in, he probably would have done.' **(Greg Downs remembers a pitch invasion at Sheffield Wednesday, 1982)**

'The lads have been crying and just sitting there. They're like zombies – but they're a great bunch.' **(First team coach Mel Machin after clinching promotion, 1982)**

'We're insured with Norwich Union, who are a particularly fine company, and we're expecting them to show that over the next few weeks.' **(City chairman Sir Arthur South reacts to the Main Stand fire, 1984)**

'Handsome…stylish defender…cultured left foot… unlucky never to have played for his country.' **(Greg Downs writes his own testimonial pen picture, 1985)**

'Garry wasn't even meant to take the penalty on Saturday. He was so quick picking up the ball and placing it on the spot that he was lining up to take it before Dixie knew what was happening. Garry had gone on and on about how he'd never missed one.' **(Ken Brown on Garry Brooke's debut penalty miss against Oldham, August 1985)**

'I always got on well with Ken Brown, but I felt he was bad at making decisions. His indecision was final, as they say.' **(Mick Channon, 1986)**

'I've already had nine different managers and I'm still only 23. You don't think they're trying to tell me anything, do you?' **(City defender Ian Butterworth, 1988)**

'Every time you see him he has a different car. He is motor-mad and likes to share that experience with everyone else on the road when he is driving.' **(Mark Bowen on Lee Power, 1992)**

'The lads call me Albert Tatlock because I'm always moaning about something or other.' **(Mark Bowen, 1992)**

'I joked that Robert Fleck was sold the previous year to pay for the new stand and I went to pay for the undersoil heating.' **(David Phillips, sold to Nottingham Forest for £500,000 in 1993)**

'Milly seems to have a different nickname every month. The latest are Mumbles because he's always moaning under his breath, and Pleaty because all the lads reckon he models his hairdo on David Pleat.' **(Ian Crook on Mike Milligan)**

'I was the only manager on *Fantasy Football League* who was fired for under-achievement.' **(Delia Smith)**

'Gary Megson gave him the nickname "Tickle" for his deft first touch.' **(Ian Crook on Spencer Prior, 1996)**

'I was exhausted going into the game. At three in the morning I was woken at our hotel by a meat delivery, from Norwich no less, and couldn't get back to sleep.' **(Keith Scott after scoring the winner at Birmingham, November 1996)**

'His tracksuits are like parachutes. We call him the Red Devil.' **(Neil Adams on Rob Newman's dress sense, 1997)**

'If I wasn't playing football I would set up a car valeting business. I love washing cars.' **(Kevin Scott, 1997)**

'I didn't say anything to him in case he told me, "I'll get my Dad on you."' **(Rob Newman has to mark Crystal Palace striker Leon McKenzie, son of boxing champion Clinton McKenzie, March 1997)**

'Martin Peters and I were talking and we stood up to let his wife Kathy in. The next thing I heard this roar go up and we'd missed the goal.' **(Kevin Keelan flies all the way from Florida, but misses Keith O'Neill's goal after just 12 seconds against Stoke, April 1997)**

'We were on tour in Scotland, we all piled into this taxi, it was about 90 degrees and Keith insisted that all the windows stayed up. He'd just done his hair.' **(Neil Adams on Keith O'Neill, 1997)**

'I decided that many of the kits are too grungy and baggy. And Delia wanted to make them more sexy to appeal to the girls.' **(Bruce Oldfield designs City's new strip, May 1997)**

'No profile would be complete without a mention of his prodigious eating ability. He has taken to the new dietary requirements of the modern game with relish – usually tomato relish.' **(Matt Jackson on Daryl Sutch, 1998)**

'We think it's a bit more upmarket where we live. We know the other place as Dustbindale.' **(City winger Adrian Forbes has Andy Marshall and Daryl Sutch as neighbours in Thorpe Marriott)**

'Peter Grant was telling me that when Dirty Den was in prison he had a picture of him on his wall. I think it's just me and him now that have been on *EastEnders*.' **(Iwan Roberts, 1999)**

'It's lovely for people to hear about but really it's a load of old garbage.' **(Manager Nigel Worthington is unimpressed with the City Academy's links with Parma)**

'It's ridiculous. I don't know where this started. I am all bloke, I can assure you. I've never worn a frock in my life. I'm the least likely man to have a sex swap.' **(Ex-City defender Tony Powell, 2004)**

'Someone's broken into your wallet, Thomas.' **(Nigel Worthington as a fire alarm interrupts new signing Thomas Helveg's first press conference, 2004)**

'He hasn't given me a copy of *In Where It Hurts* so knowing Gunny I expect he is waiting for me to buy one.' **(Nigel Worthington awaits Bryan Gunn's autobiography, 2006)**

'He writes everything down. He has a conversation and he has a little book with him all the time. He writes it down, translates it himself and five minutes later you hear him laughing to himself because he has just realised what the boys have said to each other.' **(Darel Russell on Czech striker David Strihavka, 2007)**

'They seem to have decided to put each other at each end of the running line. They've decided to cut the string between them. They've taken my advice on that. They're not running around with each other like Tweedledum and Tweedledee like they used to.' **(Glenn Roeder sees a change in Chris Martin and Michael Spillane, July 2008)**

'I'm sure there are lots of stories in different people's books that he was up to a lot of the pranks they used to do as players. But he assures me there will no longer be any hubcaps missing from the manager's wheels.' **(Bryan Gunn welcomes goalkeeping coach Paul Crichton, February 2009)**

'I can't really get to the Ashes this summer. I haven't thought of a way to get past the gaffer on that one yet.' **(Cricket fan Cody McDonald turns down tickets to Lord's because of training commitments, 2009)**

'Somebody told me some of the Walsall stewards said I had it called off. If I could get a game called off I'd part the sea as well, I think.' **(Paul Lambert, December 2009)**

'I don't know who he is but he's flown right into our area. I'm not fluent in Portuguese but if he understands Glaswegian then he might know what I said.' **(Paul Lambert reacts to Chelsea fitness coach Jose Mario Rocha encroaching in his technical area at Stamford Bridge, 2011)**

'We're Norwich City, we've come for our scarves.' **(City supporters to Manchester United's green and gold-clad fans, 2011)**

'The fear of seeing Ronald McDonald's picture every day still drives me on.' **(Striker Simeon Jackson, former McDonald's employee, January 2012)**

'The one Wes stole from me, it was St Patrick's Day and he is the Irishman in the team so I was definitely not mad as long as I got to do the Irish jig with him.' **(Kei Kamara is denied a goal at Sunderland by Wes Hoolahan's final touch, March 2013)**

(10)

The Young Ones

'I had a fantastic time at Norwich, it was just right for me. I left Bournemouth, I was a home boy, but just went to a club that was so friendly and gave me my chance in the First Division and I loved my three years there.' **(Kevin Reeves)**

'In a youth game I noticed his red hair and he looked a real scallywag tearing up and down the pitch.' **(Martin Peters on Peter Mendham)**

'There was a bit of a joke that I only played one game per season and it didn't exactly build your confidence up. I played only three first-team games up front for Norwich and it was usually when the manager had fallen out with one of his strikers.' **(Greg Downs)**

'I was quite pleased with the way it went, and I feel I did enough to justify being picked again.' **(An understated Justin Fashanu enjoys his debut against West Bromwich Albion, 1979)**

'I have had a couple of chances already this season but I suffered from an inferiority complex, being on the same field as the likes of Cyrille Regis, my idol, and was very disappointing.' **(John Fashanu, 1982)**

'I was never a nervous player before games, certainly not when I was young because you don't know what it's about and I had no fear. Ken had no fear about putting me in. I still thank him when I see him for giving me my debut.' **(Dale Gordon remembers his debut against Liverpool as a 17-year-old)**

'At the end of the week I knew that David was exactly the type of boy we wanted in our very successful youth policy at Norwich City. However, when I asked David he explained that he was already committed elsewhere. I was disappointed, to say the least, and wished him well.' **(Kit Carson, City junior football manager, tries to recruit the 12-year-old David Beckham)**

'At the time we were doing quite well and as a team we had a lot of forward players. Dion asked if we would take him on a trial basis. He did well in the reserves, scored a few goals and was certainly a skilful player, but a judgment had to be made as to whether we should increase the squad of players and therefore the wage bill.' **(Dave Stringer explains why City did not sign Dion Dublin, 18 years before they eventually did)**

'I was brought to Norwich by Kit Carson as a 14-year-old and trained with them in my summer holidays, but when the chance came to join my local club, Watford, I took it.' **(Tim Sherwood signs for City, eventually, July 1989)**

'I played for the reserves at Norwich on Friday night then drove home and went straight to bed. The first I knew about playing at Villa was when the police knocked on the door at one o'clock in the morning. I wondered what on earth had happened. I drove to Norwich at eight o'clock to pick up my boots and was then driven to Birmingham for the game. I couldn't wait to get on with it.' **(Goalkeeper Mark Walton gets an unorthodox call-up for his first team debut, April 1990)**

'To be honest, I'm not sure which position is my favourite or my best. Scoring goals puts you in the limelight but I enjoy the challenge of defending just as much.' **(An 18-year-old Chris Sutton considers his best position, 1991)**

'Lee had an excellent start but maybe in some ways it was too good a start. The novelty can wear off after half a dozen games.' **(City manager Mike Walker on striker Lee Power, 1992)**

'I can be very cocky but I can also be very nice.' **(Craig Bellamy, 1997)**

'He's only been in the building three weeks and he's already pushing for a reserve team place.' **(City youth team boss Keith Webb rates the 16-year-old Darel Russell, 1997)**

'He's rubbed a few people up the wrong way but if he wasn't such a good player you wouldn't put up with it.' **(Mike Walker on Craig Bellamy, who at 17 dubbed himself the new Juninho)**

'Craig was a handful in and around the dressing room, but one thing that always shone through was his love of the game.' **(Matt Jackson on former City team-mate Craig Bellamy)**

'I think some of my friends get a bit jealous because we play football and I have a bit more money. It's a bit awkward, really.' **(Chris Llewellyn, 1997)**

'I slept well last night. I was very settled and calm. I'm a very laid-back person, almost horizontal.' **(Robert Green is not worried by his City debut against Ipswich, 1999)**

'At Manchester United in the reserves, knowing you were maybe only going to get a game once every two or three weeks, I found it very difficult to get myself worked up for it. Now everything is a challenge.' **(New signing Phil Mulryne, 1999)**

'It was a large part of my life to be there and I put a lot of work in there – as a place to grow up as a person and learn your football it was a tremendous experience.' **(Robert Green)**

'I enjoyed it even though we got relegated. It was very difficult. We were losing and you can underperform, but it shapes you as a player and a person and I learnt a lot about myself.' **(David Bentley on his season at Norwich, 2005)**

'He's the first one to know there's been a lot of talk about talent, ability, this, that and the other. It's now time to really show that. He's got it so go and express it and we've got to pick him. There will be times when he's in, times when he's out.' **(Nigel Worthington on Ryan Jarvis, September 2006)**

'He looks like one of these boys who in years to come could captain this club. There's no doubt about that in my mind if he keeps progressing the way he is.' **(Peter Grant's verdict on Jason Shackell after one match in charge, October 2006)**

'I suppose it can be that the attractions and the bright lights lead people astray, but you can't afford to let your mind get sidetracked by cars, women and whatever else you care to mention.' **(Striker Chris Martin, October 2009)**

'I was 16 when I got released from Ipswich. My mate was at Norwich, Tom Miller, and I came here for a couple of weeks' training but nothing came of it and that's when I ended up going straight to Grimsby.' **(Ryan Bennett joins City for £3m, five years after an unsuccessful trial, 2012)**

(11)

League Cup By Any Other Name

'We beat Blackpool in the semi-final because I played against Jimmy Armfield. Years later, I remember seeing Jimmy at Wembley because he presented the FA Vase to Diss when we won it. "I'm glad I don't have to mark you today," he said.' **(City winger Bill Punton on the 1962 League Cup win)**

'We had to play eight games and we did really well to win it. I remember getting a £4 bonus for winning it.' **(Bill Punton on a lucrative League Cup Final success)**

'Whatever happens to the League Cup – its mere existence is in the balance – this will go down as one of the most disappointing finals there has been of a national competition.' **(David Dunn, *Eastern Evening News*, on City's 1962 victory over Rochdale)**

'I scored a hat-trick, Charlie Crickmore scored one. We had all the board of directors on the bus and Danny Blanchflower, who was working for Anglia Television and his television crew, were there all the way there and all the way back. Ipswich had just been promoted to the First Division, so with us in the Second Division, that was double the glory so to speak.' **(Hugh Curran remembers City's 4-2 League Cup win at Ipswich, 1968)**

'We told the referee that he could see all right. Chelsea told him it was impossible. He told us all that he was in charge and he would make the decision. In the end he had no choice, but what a rotten way to be robbed.' **(Doug Livermore after the semi-final second leg against Chelsea is abandoned through fog, with City 5-2 ahead on aggregate, 1972)**

'Suddenly through the fog I could see David Webb of Chelsea running towards me. I thought, "God, where's the ball?" and was ready to throw myself at him when he shouted, "Come on Kev, we've gone off."' **(Kevin Keelan, *The Story of a Goalkeeper*, recalls the abandoned game against Chelsea, 1972)**

'Everyone was stunned, and when the referee and players went off – by this time even the centre circle was barely discernible – no one knew what was happening. There was chaos in the press box. A huge crowd was pressed around the box standing and wondering and metaphorically gnashing its teeth in anguish.' **(Bruce Robinson, *Passing Seasons,* on the abandoned semi-final)**

'The cruellest night in Norwich City's history. I feel so upset for the players, the manager and the supporters. It's a tragic disappointment.' **(Chairman Geoffrey Watling after fog postpones City's celebrations, 1972)**

'Peter Osgood was an excellent player on his day when he concentrated on his football. He hit me right across the Adam's apple as we ran out after Kevin Keelan caught a cross.' **(Match-winner Steve Govier recalls a bruising semi-final replay against Chelsea, 1973)**

'Osgood came back with me for the corner. I'd beaten him most times in the air and as soon as he jumped I thought he went too soon. He was on the way down as I came up and I headed it in, but I didn't even see it go in.' **(Steve Govier on his winning goal against Chelsea, 1973)**

'They've got between now and March to sort out the league. By the time they start training again they will have forgotten all about Wembley.' **(Ron Saunders, moments after City clinched their League Cup Final place, 1973)**

'Ron Saunders told me to go and talk to Sheffield United. I asked him at the time, "If I decide not to go does that mean I will play in the final?" He said there were no guarantees. I took it from that that he didn't want me to stay. It was awful timing. Jimmy Blair took my place at Wembley but he was a completely different type of player to me.' **(Jim Bone, transferred to Sheffield United on the eve of the 1973 League Cup Final)**

'Jim Bone was sold in the week before the final, but Ron Saunders played Jim Blair in the final instead of me. Jim was a nice fella and when the teamsheet went up I was the first to shake his hand, but I was gutted. I think I cried all the way through the game but I was only 19 and I wasn't experienced enough to deal with it.' **(Paul Cheesley misses out on Wembley, 1973)**

'That winner was tremendous. It must rank as my best goal for Spurs.' **(Tottenham substitute Ralph Coates, 1973 League Cup Final match-winner against City)**

'We can be proud of every one of our team in this final. It was a physical game but never dirty. The goal came against the run of play when we were getting on top.' **(City boss Ron Saunders, League Cup Final, 1973)**

'We just froze, I think. I certainly did. I remember feeling drained as "God Save the Queen" was coming on. And I looked at some of the other lads. I looked along the line and wondered if everyone feels like I do.' **(David Cross on City's Wembley defeat, 1973)**

'Nobody wants to know the losers. I remember at the end that the band played Cliff Richard's song, "Congratulations". Every time I hear it, it reminds me and I think, "Oh, switch that off!"' **(Dave Stringer on City's Wembley defeat, 1973)**

'Super Ted came over to me singing the David Essex song "We're Gonna Make You a Star". After I scored I waved to my landlady and her husband, Edith and Roy Blenkinsop, who sat in the Main Stand, to say thank you for looking after me like a son.' **(Steve Goodwin's League Cup double sinks Sheffield United, 1974)**

'I scooped the ball on to the post. My body was over the line but not the ball. I don't know how the linesman could see because my body must have obscured his view.' **(Kevin Keelan on Trevor Whymark's controversial quarter-final goal for Ipswich, December 1974)**

'This gave me the greatest satisfaction of my career. I may even pop out for a small drink to celebrate.' **(City winger John Miller scores twice in 2-1 win at former club Ipswich in League Cup quarter-final replay, December 1974)**

Colin Suggett suffered Wembley woe: 'We had players who were not 100 per cent fit.'

Kevin Keelan cost £6,500. 'Some people thought it was too much to spend,' said Ron Ashman.

Glenn Roeder famously labelled two of his City squad as Tweedledum and Tweedledee.

Bryan Gunn urged referee Andy D'Urso to dig out his DVD player.

Iwan Roberts said he would 'die a happy man' with 100 goals for City. He scored 96.

Kevin Drinkell with fellow striker John Deehan, the keen angler who 'didn't expect to be used as bait'.

Mel Machin and Ken Brown with the Milk Cup in 1985. 'There are no words to describe the feeling,' said Brown.

Steve Bruce, complete with hat, admitted the Milk Cup party 'went on a bit too long'.

Sunderland's Clive Walker misses his Milk Cup final penalty. 'It took me years to get over it.'

Winning skipper Dave Watson on the first of many outings at Wembley.

City were Division Two champions in 1986. 'At least we got back at the first attempt,' said Ken Brown.

Lee Croft knew why City were relegated in 2009. 'Because we haven't won enough games to be out of the bottom three.'

Darren Huckerby was denied a farewell in 2008.

Peter Grant wanted 'Celtic and Norwich' on his gravestone.

Don't mention Parma to Nigel Worthington.

Darel Russell saw red seven times with City.

Delia Smith 'fell in love with Graham Paddon and his blond hair'.

Paul Lambert and Grant Holt both tipped City for promotion after the Colchester debacle.

Not much worried Robert Green. 'I'm a very laid-back person, almost horizontal.'

Wes Hoolahan danced an Irish jig after scoring on St Patrick's Day.

'I think Ron Saunders has an awful lot of ability in his team. Even though it will be two Second Division sides at Wembley, it could turn out to be a very good final.' **(John Bond looks ahead to the final against Aston Villa, 1975)**

'Wembley is a lonely place to lose at. People say that losing the semi-final is worse but they're wrong. When you lose at Wembley and see the other team dancing about and celebrating, it's terrible.' **(Duncan Forbes, who skippered City in two League Cup Final defeats)**

'We had been on a good run of form but a few of the boys had been injured and hadn't trained for a while. We had players who were not 100 per cent fit. Mel Machin and Johnny Miller were not fully fit. I suppose it was a one-off chance to play at Wembley and it was decided to play them but it didn't help the rest of the team.' **(Colin Suggett on City's 1-0 League Cup Final defeat by Aston Villa)**

'Playing both Mel Machin and Johnny Miller was a calculated risk – and it didn't come off. Machin aggravated his thigh injury with the first kick of the game and I don't know how long he'll be out.' **(John Bond admits his Wembley team selection was a mistake, 1975)**

'We were absolute rubbish. In the second half it was a slaughter, kids against men. There are three things I can't stand – getting beaten, being embarrassed, being humiliated. All three happened to me in that match. It has been a shattering experience.' **(John Bond on City's Wembley defeat, 1975)**

'I'd never seen Graydon take a penalty so I decided to gamble and go to my right. Just how close I was to saving the shot will haunt me for the rest of my life. The ball could have gone anywhere off that post and if it had bounced away I'm sure we'd have held out for a replay. When Graydon got the rebound and scored, it was the worst moment of my football career.' **(City goalkeeper Kevin Keelan recalls Villa's Wembley winner)**

'I thought we could get a draw despite playing so badly, and then have a chance to turn it on in the replay.' **(Ted MacDougall on defeat at Wembley, 1975)**

'When Bond said he would have no sympathy for me if Villa lost, he was talking about something he doesn't understand. I've got sympathy for the Norwich players, their wives, relatives, friends – and their manager. I have lost twice at Wembley.' **(Aston Villa manager Ron Saunders, 1975)**

'I am unable to smoke big cigars like some managers.' **(Ron Saunders, 1975)**

'Butch Wilkins said to me, "I reckon you were pleased with that one" and yes, I was very pleased. I was better known for stopping goals than scoring them.' **(Phil Hoadley scores his only City goal in a 4-1 League Cup win over Manchester United, 1979)**

'I actually travelled back on the coach with the Preston team because I was living at Wilmslow at the time. We'd beaten them 6-1 so I don't know if I was very popular on the bus. It was quite strange.' **(Asa Hartford scores twice on his Milk Cup debut, then goes home with the losing team, 1984)**

'I've sent my spare standing tickets to unfashionable Norwich because they couldn't find enough. I've been pulled apart with requests from Sunderland fans who haven't filled their ground for some years.' **(Brian Clough looks ahead to the 1985 Milk Cup Final)**

'With the game being played on the Sunday it made it the same day as my birthday, which was extra special. There was a whole week of build-up but the game itself flew by. The older players said to us, "This will pass you by in a flash" and that was exactly right. Blink and it was gone.' **(Paul Haylock recalls the 1985 Milk Cup Final)**

'Just getting there, beating our East Anglian rivals Ipswich Town 2-0 in the second leg of the semi-final, was an unforgettable occasion. Dixie Deehan and Steve Bruce got the goals then, and we were carried off shoulder high. That didn't even happen when I was with Southampton and we beat Manchester United for the FA Cup.' **(Mick Channon on Milk Cup success, 1985)**

'I think Terry Butcher was supposed to be picking me up and I just managed to wriggle free of him. The kick from Mark Barham came in fairly flat and I knew my head was on it. After that, the place went crazy – with Ipswich being our big local derby.' **(Steve Bruce on his Milk Cup semi-final winner against Ipswich)**

'Next year we're going to win the FA Cup because it's too bloody cold at this time of year.' **(Mick Channon on the Milk Cup winners' parade, 1985)**

'I was there in 1976 when Newcastle Boys provided the ball boys for the League Cup Final against Manchester City and I was one of them.' **(Steve Bruce remembers his first Wembley visit)**

'Whatever happens, my intention is to retire in four years' time, when I'm 55.' **(Ken Brown plans ahead at the 1985 Milk Cup Final)**

'There are no words to describe the feeling. I'd played an international, I'd played for my club but to lead your own team out in a final, well, that was special. That was quite a hat-trick.' **(Ken Brown returns to Wembley, 1985)**

'John Deehan did really well chasing a lost cause and when the ball came to me I hit it and it hit Gordon Chisholm and went in. It seemed to be my goal but it was only when Sunderland lined up to kick off again that I looked up at the scoreboard and it said "Chisholm own goal". I thought I was going to see my name up in lights!' **(Asa Hartford on his Milk Cup winning goal, 1985)**

'I always fancied myself because I had a pretty sweet left foot. I fancied myself that day and thought I hit it pretty well, but the ball clipped the post. It took me years to get over it. I was off penalties for ages. That is how badly affected I was.' **(Sunderland's Clive Walker on his Wembley penalty miss)**

'I'm going to give my medal to my six-month-old son, Alex.' **(Steve Bruce at Wembley, 1985)**

'This is better than anything I have known in my time at any club. It's a once-in-a-lifetime thing.' **(Asa Hartford on winning the Milk Cup, 1985)**

'The whole Wembley day was most enjoyable, not playing there before. The problem was the party went on a bit too long and we got relegated.' **(Steve Bruce)**

'There are mixed memories because we were not allowed to go into Europe and we were very disappointed to get relegated. That made it hurt more, one thing after the other. Perhaps we took our eye off the ball, perhaps we eased off somewhere along the line, but at least we got back at the first attempt.' **(Ken Brown on the aftermath of the 1985 Milk Cup Final)**

'We'd be extremely disappointed if we didn't go through now.' **(Ian Crook after a 6-1 Coca-Cola Cup first leg home win over Torquay, 1995)**

(12)

Nice To Meet You, Mr Bond

'Norwich are not third from bottom of the First Division because they are the best side in the land.' **(John Bond takes over as City manager, November 1973)**

'John Bond arrived at Carrow Road on a Tuesday and I was a Bournemouth player by the Saturday. I didn't want to leave but Bond made it clear I did not figure in his plans.' **(City full-back Clive Payne)**

'A first-minute goal can sometimes be too early. You start thinking you have 89 minutes to hold out.' **(John Bond after a 1-1 draw against Liverpool, December 1973)**

'I know lots of people in the city are finding it difficult to understand why I have bought so many players from my old club, Bournemouth. The first reason is that I think they are good players.' **(John Bond, 1974)**

'John Bond was an extrovert but I didn't really like his attitude towards the players who were already at the club. I thought he was disrespectful and almost tried to belittle some of them. He brought about seven players in from Bournemouth but the players he inherited still got us to the League Cup semi-final, where we lost to Wolves.' **(Ex-City winger Ian Mellor)**

'All good sides in the First Division have two good players up front – like Richards and Dougan at Wolves – and now we have it here with MacDougall and Boyer. These two complement each other splendidly, and I suppose the contrast in personalities is one of the reasons.' **(John Bond, February 1974)**

'My father brought Harry to Norwich and I played in the reserves with him, so he knows the place himself, though not quite like I do.' **(Kevin Bond remembers Harry Redknapp's three games in City colours)**

'He is unfortunate that a top club did not sign him from Bournemouth. He could have been an England player. Spurs and Crystal Palace both showed an interest but they never moved in. Looking back, they must have been mad.' **(John Bond on Mel Machin, October 1974)**

'Most people thought I would be the first to go when John Bond arrived, and I must confess to surprise and gratitude at being given the chance to survive. Even a Bond team can carry a bit of steel, and presumably he has seen me as one of the players to provide it.' **(Skipper Duncan Forbes, 1975)**

'I played against the boss and Ken Brown when they were at Torquay. It wasn't hard to take defensive honours while the old men were on parade.' **(Full-back Colin Sullivan, 1975)**

'Training under John Bond was nearly all with the ball and the players really enjoyed what was put on for them. That takes nothing away from what Ron Saunders achieved but they just used two different techniques. With

Ron, it was run until you drop.' **(Steve Grapes, 1970s winger)**

'Bondy was very helpful, he would say anything and do anything – he'd even tell you his team on a Tuesday.' **(Gerry Harrison, *Match of the Week* commentator)**

'It's like a breath of fresh air coming to Norwich.' **(Martin Peters joins City, March 1975)**

'You can never blame a man for missing a penalty. I'll warrant he nets another dozen before he misses again.' **(John Bond on Ted MacDougall's failed spot-kick against Fulham, 1975)**

'Bondy got us all playing and my time at Norwich was my best in football.' **(City midfielder Colin Suggett)**

'My sincere hope for 1976 is that enough people in the game will come to terms with the most obvious requirement – to entertain the spectators. This is basically show business.' **(John Bond, December 1975)**

'I know many people will say bigmouth Bond is sounding off again, but I assure you this has nothing to do with sour grapes. There was only one team out there today trying to play the game the right way. Away from home, Liverpool stifle and hope for a break and they are boring the crowds. They got two points today and good luck to them, but it saddens me and worries me.' **(John Bond is critical of Liverpool's style, March 1976)**

'I walked down these corridors for 17 years and it means an awful lot to me to come back today and win. The team talk was one of the easiest I have ever had to give. I just told the players I wanted a win for myself.' **(John Bond after a 1-0 win at West Ham, March 1976)**

'People don't realise that Ted is one of the game's great thinkers. He can see space and use it before anyone else knows it's there.' **(John Bond on Ted MacDougall, 1976)**

'He probably gets more stick at this club than any other player in training, in the dressing room and out on the pitch. A lot of it's from me.' **(John Bond on son Kevin, 1977)**

'If Chivers proves only half as good an investment as Martin Peters was, then I shall be well pleased.' **(John Bond signs Martin Chivers from Servette, 1978)**

'City managers have been criticised in the past for being too parochial in their outlook, but that criticism could never be levelled at John Bond. He is looking to learn from international football all the time and feels that European soccer would be the best thing ever to happen for Norwich City.' **(Richard Futter, 1978)**

'This contract will take me up to the age of 55 and I'm delighted. We started a youth scheme here and now it looks as if we are getting the rewards. I'm going to stay and see it through.' **(John Bond gets a new nine-year contract, November 1978)**

'I took a chance when I bought him from the Swiss club Servette. The fee was minute in terms of present-day transfers and it was a chance I was prepared to take, including allowing him to live in London, and that is not working out well.' **(John Bond puts Martin Chivers on the transfer list, January 1979)**

'John Bond asked me if I'd do a man-to-man marking job on Ossie Ardiles and I said, "No problem." He never got a kick and we drew 0-0. He got taken off after an hour or so and Peter Taylor came on.' **(Doug Evans helps subdue a World Cup winner, 1979)**

'Football and television are natural partners and will go on living together when we are all gone.' **(John Bond, 1979)**

'Sometimes I wonder where I would be without him. Now it looks as if we will be together all our football lives.' **(John Bond on assistant manager Ken Brown, 1979)**

'One of John Bond's greatest talents has been this tremendous gift to make people want to play for him. I think that in general the players like him. Most of them realise that underneath that bluff exterior which he often adopts for the media is a warm, kind-hearted and generous man with a great sense of humour.' **(Kevin Keelan, *Story of a Goalkeeper*, 1979)**

'I honestly believe Kevin Reeves will develop into another Kevin Keegan, and there is no higher praise because Keegan is one of the world's greats.' **(John Bond, August 1979)**

'The first time he played me in a five-a-side in training, he told me, "I'm letting you play this one but if you don't go out and get your hair cut you won't be playing another one."' **(Mark Barham gets a warning from John Bond)**

'Norwich's goal was scored by Kevin Bond, who is the son of his father.' **(Frank Bough)**

'I was trying to stir him up. I know he hadn't felt well earlier in the week, but that was no excuse for not battling at a critical point in the game. He was playing awfully and I said that for two pins I would have taken him off and played with ten men.' **(John Bond slams son Kevin after 5-3 home defeat by Liverpool, 1980)**

'I am looking forward to carrying on my job with Norwich City for a long, long time.' **(John Bond, September 1980, one month before resigning)**

'I haven't actually seen him play but I would have thought his record of 36 caps speaks for itself.' **(John Bond signs Yugoslavia international Drazen Muzinic for a club record £300,000, August 1980)**

'Bondy signed me and very quickly lost faith – that's what he told me after two or three games, that he had made a mistake.' **(Joe Royle, who still became player of the season, 1980/81)**

'I did it to take the nervousness away from Roger. Instead of a nervous build-up, he came into the dressing room thinking he wasn't playing, and when I told him he was he had no time to get worried and was determined to make the most of his opportunity. It worked, didn't it? Roger was superb.' **(John Bond 'drops' Roger Hansbury for a League Cup replay against Ipswich but reprieves him, 1980)**

'They don't seem to want me near the place.' **(John Bond, October 1980, after his Jaguar is reclaimed by the club)**

'Right now I would rather play for Reading or Doncaster Rovers than I would for Norwich. The only way I would consider changing my mind would be if the chairman was to leave. If I do well for them I am doing well for the chairman, and I don't want that to happen because of the way he treated my father.' **(Kevin Bond asks for a transfer, October 1980)**

'Despite all his problems – sometimes his attitude and sometimes his manner towards the press – he was a first-class manager. I think perhaps he had outgrown the city.

He left us with a team that was beginning to struggle.' **(Chairman Sir Arthur South on John Bond, 1981)**

'I didn't sign so much for John Bond, because I did not know the man, as for the club. But immediately I did not get on with the man, and it wasn't all that long before I was back at Carrow Road.' **(Martin O'Neill on his brief stay with Manchester City, 1982)**

'One thing we did that other regions didn't was speak to the manager before the game and again at half-time. Nobody else did. There was one incident when Norwich were playing Wolves and were 2-0 down at half-time. When the second half started, straightaway Wolves scored again and there was this cry from Bondy before he threw the headphones and microphone off.' **(Gerry Harrison, *Match of the Week* commentator)**

'John Bond wanted to play football. He did much more on forward play than he did with the defensive play, even though he was a full-back in his playing days and his assistant, Ken Brown, was a centre-half. Bondy knew he had two players who could score goals.' **(Duncan Forbes)**

'What John Bond didn't know about football could be written on the back of a postage stamp.' **(Mark Barham, September 2012)**

'John was a great character. He said what he thought and, at times, he riled people, but he was honest and felt he had to say what he felt had to be said, you always knew where you were with him.' **(Ken Brown tribute on the death of John Bond, 2012)**

(13)

It's All About The Players

'We were great mates and rivals. There was no ill feeling between us at all. I remember we used to go to the pictures together most weeks.' **(Ken Oxford on fellow City goalkeeper Ken Nethercott)**

'I was first and foremost a winger but they let me rove all over the place. I was an aggressive sort of winger, always in the thick of the action.' **(City's record goalscorer Johnny Gavin)**

'Errol was as quick as anybody I've ever seen or played with. He had a strange running gait with his knees coming up high a bit like the sprinter Michael Johnson. I knew that if I played a ball behind the full-back he would get it. He made some of my passes look good.' **(Terry Allcock on winger Errol Crossan)**

'All the skill was there but maybe we attacked too much. We also had one or two "homer" type players who when they went away just didn't seem to perform the same.' **(Ollie Burton on City's early 1960s side)**

'I have lost a very good friend for I lived closer to Barry perhaps than to any other player during the time I've been with Norwich City. I shared rooms with him at away games and we often shared our problems as well. I can't believe it has happened. I feel perhaps I shall miss him even more now because he would have worked with me as player-coach.' **(Manager Ron Ashman on the death of club captain Barry Butler, April 1966)**

'Kevin was brilliant. He wasn't the best trainer in the world. He liked a pint and he smoked. But put him between the posts and he was out of this world, and he was a smashing bloke.' **(Peter Vasper on fellow goalkeeper Kevin Keelan)**

'Ted had a marvellous scoring record over the years, especially in the First Division with Norwich. But he was not the best person to play with because he was so demanding. If you didn't put it exactly where he wanted you knew you would get it in the neck. Everything had to go around Ted, but off the pitch he was a great fella.' **(Ex-City winger Steve Grapes on Ted MacDougall)**

'Duncan was first-class in every way. People were a little bit surprised when Ron Saunders left that he was still the first name on the team sheet, because John Bond liked to get the ball down and play, but he knew he would get 200 per cent out of the guy every game.' **(Steve Grapes on Duncan Forbes)**

'Martin was a very underestimated player. I played against him when he was at Spurs, but it was only when you trained with him every day and played with him every week that you realised just how good he was. He was a wonderful goalscorer, a great header of the ball, and a great penalty taker but he was also very tough and could look after himself.' **(Colin Suggett on Martin Peters)**

'I saw Terry the next day, going to buy the newspapers with his name on all the back pages.' **(David Cross is delighted by Terry Anderson's two goals in a 3-2 win over his former club, Arsenal, 1972)**

'I need something outside the game, and learning to play the piano is one of those satisfying hobbies that is really worthwhile.' **(Mick McGuire, 1975)**

'Of course I'm very sad, although I knew it had to come sooner or later. Perhaps reactions are that split second slower, while I haven't been so good in the air, normally the strong point of my game. There have been some poor team performances and as captain I expected a bigger rap than some of the others.' **(Duncan Forbes is dropped by manager John Bond, September 1976)**

'It was a joy to play alongside Martin Peters. He did all the playing, I did all the running.' **(John Ryan, player of the season 1977/78)**

'I thoroughly enjoyed my time at Norwich. They were two of the best years of my football career and I learned a lot from John Bond. I also seemed to have a good rapport with the crowd. They seemed to know I was a 100-per-center.' **(Striker Roger Gibbins)**

'I wish I had had the same faith in myself that John Bond had in me. I was a nervous guy and wasn't one of those people who went out for a game relaxed and totally confident.' **(Ex-City goalkeeper Roger Hansbury)**

'Most players in the league have earned their positions due to their skill factor. With me it is not so much skill as will.' **(Jeremy Goss, 1988)**

'I had two lovely years at Norwich. A knee injury did for me in the end but in my only full season I won the player of the year award – the only one I won at any of my clubs. It was very nice and I'm very proud of it.' **(Joe Royle)**

'I took a bit of stick from the crowd but I never hid. I always wanted the ball and I wasn't prepared just to hoof it forward aimlessly.' **(Mick McGuire)**

'A lot of it was paper talk. Everybody looks for their home team's result, don't they?' **(Winger Clive Woods on being a Norwich fan in the Ipswich dressing room)**

'If you are going to be bringing people down just for the sake of stopping them getting through, or handling the ball, you are just going to frustrate the fans and drive people away.' **(Centre-half Willie Young, 1983)**

'Those six months on the dole were terrible. But I kept faith that I might one day get back into full-time football. Every morning I got up early and trained hard by myself before looking for work.' **(Striker Wayne Biggins, March 1986)**

'The gulf between the standard of football here and at Watford is immense.' **(City midfielder Tim Sherwood, 1991)**

'Every time I read anything about myself in the papers, I seem to be described as a utility man, and to be honest I hate it. It makes it seem as though you are a Jack of all trades and master of none.' **(Full-back Colin Woodthorpe, 1992)**

'I've always thought of myself as a right-footed player. It's just that I had to play on the left side of midfield in the reserves at Spurs and I got in at left-back when Chris Hughton was injured. From then on it just sort of stuck.' **(Full-back Mark Bowen, 1992)**

'When John Deehan gave me the captain's armband and told me I was the record signing, it filled me with confidence. He put his arm round me and said he wanted me to be an integral part of the club. I wanted to repay the manager and I think that's why I played some of my best football for Norwich. I never really felt as big a part of a club before.' **(Jon Newsome)**

'Even playing in the League Cup Final and FA Cup semi-finals with Oldham, and playing for Everton, Norwich was the best footballing side I played in and it was a delight.' **(Mike Milligan)**

'I do regret not winning anything. It certainly wasn't my first ambition when I moved here but as the years have gone by I do regret not ever having the chance to play at Wembley.' **(Ian Crook, 1995)**

'When I came to Norwich, I was given extra responsibilities in central midfield, and I feel those responsibilities spurred me on and brought out the best in me.' **(Martin O'Neill)**

'It was one of the finest moments of my life. There wasn't a dry eye in the house.' **(City defender Rob Newman on his saxophone solo 'Misty' at his wedding)**

'I've played against Iwan a number of times. He's big, strong, holds the ball up well and works that channel very well.' **(Skipper Matt Jackson welcomes new signing Iwan Roberts, 1997)**

'Now on my gravestone I will have "Peter Grant – Celtic and Norwich".' **(Grant signs for City, 1997)**

'If I was released by Norwich I would try every other club except Ipswich.' **(Adrian Coote, Norfolk born and bred, 1998)**

'It was a little bit daunting at first and I flapped at the first cross, but as the game went on I grew in confidence.' **(Defender Daryl Sutch plays more than 80 minutes in goal at Huddersfield, March 1999)**

'My brother is working with the Corporation in Dublin and I used to slog my butt off working in a computer warehouse all day long.' **(Brian McGovern, 2001)**

'I get a buzz out of proving people wrong. People have always doubted my ability to move up a level.' **(Leon McKenzie, 2004)**

'If anyone had said to me when I first came here on loan that we'd win the title and I'd be named Division One player of the season, I'd never have believed them. It's worked out quite well.' **(Darren Huckerby, 2004)**

'I'm not the type of player that's going to be piling in for headers and putting myself about. I was always going to go to a club that looks to pass the ball.' **(David Bentley signs on loan, 2004)**

'I just love playing football. Ask anyone who knows me and they'll tell you the same – that if I wasn't playing for Norwich or whoever, then I'd still be looking to play at park level.' **(Robert Green, 2005)**

'I've been doing it for ten years. I just fancied the idea of it and picked up a board. It seems a bit strange for a bloke from Manchester to be a surfer but it certainly keeps you fit.' **(Peter Thorne, 2005)**

'A lot of people have said, "Do you enjoy playing up front on your own?" The thing people forget is, if you get the support around you, you're almost playing a front five.' **(Robert Earnshaw, 2006)**

'What do I remember about Norwich? I had a bad time and the fans never took to me. I never did what I was signed to do, which was score goals. I hold my hands up to that. The injuries didn't help when I was trying to prove myself, but that's life and you just have to crack on.' **(Ex-City striker Dean Coney, 2006)**

'We do have a few scuffles now and again. He came back from training the other day and he caught me on the ankle and we had a little scuffle, but everyone does that. It's not just brothers.' **(Ryan Jarvis on Rossi Jarvis, first brothers to appear in the City first team together for 78 years, September 2006)**

'I had so many firsts at Carrow Road in my career. Norwich was my first English club, my first game as Bournemouth player-assistant boss was here in the Worthington Cup, I was here with West Ham on the day the Jarrold Stand was opened for the first time and now it's my first job in management. So much so I've been asked if it was my destiny to manage this club.' **(Peter Grant, October 2006)**

'It's funny that no one actually sees that on match day, but that's football. Nobody actually sees the hard work that some players put in. It doesn't bother me. I know I'm a fit lad.' **(Dickson Etuhu runs nearly 12km per game for City, 2007)**

'I'm very pleased to be re-signing for a club I feel very at home with. I hope next season can be the successful one we all want, as the last one wasn't. We have the potential but we have to stop talking about it and do it.' **(Dion Dublin signs up for one last season, May 2007)**

'Chris Sutton was probably the best player in my time at the club. He made a huge difference for us.' **(Ian Crook, 2008)**

'I believe there is no better left-winger in the division. I've played with him, trained with him every day and seen his ability on the ball, his final ball. And he has the mentality and confidence to do well. You need a bit about you to play for Norwich and they would like a player with his ability.' **(Adrian Forbes on former Blackpool team-mate Wes Hoolahan, 2008)**

'I'm not a legend. I never won anything with Norwich apart from player of the year. You have to look at people like Dave Stringer and Duncan Forbes or the team that won the Milk Cup.' **(Robert Fleck, 2008)**

'I think sometimes footballers say stupid things at times. They don't really think about what they're saying.' **(Loan striker David Mooney, 2009)**

'The manager didn't really need to sell the club to me. I would probably have walked from Devon.' **(Matthew Gill signs from Exeter, June 2009)**

'I don't try to complicate things. I head it and kick it when it needs to be and try to dominate the centre-forward I'm playing against.' **(Michael Nelson signs for City, 2009)**

'I'm quite religious, Catholic, so my whole left arm is based on that really. The other side seems to be a bit more of my bad side – I'm sort of split down the middle.' **(Jamie Cureton describes his tattoos, 2009)**

'Out on the training pitch you get to do more tricks, but in a game you limit yourself because you don't want to make any mistakes.' **(Wes Hoolahan, October 2009)**

'If Ian Crook can't coach people then I don't know who can because he was technically one of the finest players I've seen and it was a privilege to play and train with him.' **(Colin Woodthorpe)**

'If you had nine or ten like him in the side you wouldn't go far wrong.' **(Iwan Roberts on new City signing and former Gillingham club-mate Andrew Crofts, 2010)**

'I'm big so I like to win a few headers and defend first. I have to head it, kick it, put my body in front of the ball, but once the defending's done if there's time I like to try to play football as well.' **(Elliott Ward joins City, 2010)**

'My brother writes plays and directs them – he played Macbeth at Shoreditch last year and we went down to see it and he was brilliant. I was so proud of him. He said to me, "That's exactly how I feel when I come to watch you play."' **(Russell Martin, 2010)**

'I just prepare for every game as if I am going to play, so nothing changed. I did everything the way I normally do – a quiet night in on Friday and bed at five past 12 after all the celebrations.' **(Zak Whitbread has a quiet New Year's Eve, 2010)**

'I'd play Saturday-Tuesday every week if we could. I'm pretty young, 26, I love playing every game. Thick and fast is the way I love it.' **(Andrew Crofts, April 2011)**

'It's a weird one. When you look at the names on the trophy and look at the people who have been through this club as players, it's ridiculous. I'm sure it will sink in at some point, but not now.' **(Grant Holt wins the player of the season award for the third time running, May 2012)**

'Going down to Norwich, you're straightaway involved in a relegation battle and the mindset changed overnight. One minute, I was a young player who was in the shadow of the big players and next thing I was starting every game and was being relied upon. I was only 22 and it was the making of me.' **(Goalkeeper David Marshall)**

(14)

Boardroom Battles

'I don't feel like being a member of a set-up gang. The man in the street is not getting a fair crack of the whip because the whole thing is cut and dried.' **(City Supporters' Club president Len Votier drops out of the nominations for the new board, 1957)**

'You will either accept the ruling of the chairman or leave the meeting.' **(Lord Mayor of Norwich, Arthur South, deals with an angry shareholder at the club's extraordinary general meeting, 1957)**

'Let's cut the cackle and get on with the job. If we don't pull round it won't be for the want of trying. I can't do it alone, nor can the board.' **(Geoffrey Watling becomes City chairman, 1957)**

'Some meetings go wrong, some right, and this one went right from the start. And I had some good lieutenants. You got the feeling that everybody was there to support you and wanted the club to survive.' **(Arthur South recalls the club's extraordinary general meeting, 1957)**

'The directors were hyper-critical if anything went wrong. I thought my team was playing quite well but I was getting criticism all the time.' **(George Swindin, City manager for just 20 games, 1962)**

'Three years ago for various reasons I thought I had held office long enough but decided to continue and achieved my great ambition – promotion to the First Division. Now I have given the matter serious and careful thought and have reluctantly decided not to accept the chairmanship for the coming season.' **(Chairman Geoffrey Watling resigns, annual meeting 1973)**

'Everyone knows him as Citizen South of Norwich. Now he is Citizen South of Norwich City Football Club.' **(Geoffrey Watling hails his successor as chairman, 1973)**

'Those members of the board who were not present at the away game at Wolverhampton on Easter Monday have received a report of an outrageous outburst and conduct by the chairman to a fellow director in the private boardroom of the Wolverhampton club, and in the presence of the chairman and directors of that club. Offensive language, including gross obscenities and profanities were shouted by Sir Arthur South at one of his fellow directors.' **(Directors' statement, April 1976)**

'Henry Robinson called at my business and said to me, "We have had a meeting and you should know we have no confidence in you and there is no point having a board meeting tonight because we want you to resign."' **(Chairman Sir Arthur South faces a revolt by fellow directors, 1976)**

'I remember Ron Ashman saying we should all have a good cry when we went out to Luton in 1959. I feel the same way now. It's a tragedy.' **(City president James Hanly on the Carrow Road fire, 1984)**

'It is beyond my understanding how Luton, or any other football club, can expect their members and supporters to come to Carrow Road, but when we go there, say that our City Stand members, season ticket-holders and other supporters will be barred entry. I think football has scored another own goal with this terrible publicity.' **(Chairman Robert Chase reacts to Luton's away fan ban, September 1986)**

'It was because of poor results that Ken Brown and the club parted company. Ken Brown forced us to sack him and the privileges you normally receive after resigning he has, I am afraid, lost.' **(Robert Chase, extraordinary general meeting, 18 January, 1988)**

'There is nobody more aware than your directors of the service Ken Brown has given this club for many years. But it is irresponsible to allow sentiment to affect decisions.' **(Robert Chase, extraordinary general meeting, 18 January 1988)**

'We have satisfied all the requirements of the Taylor Report and, what is more important, we have done so within the timescale which enabled us to take advantage of every element of the grant aid available to us.' **(Robert Chase as Carrow Road goes all-seater, 1992)**

'In Martin O'Neill I believe we have the ideal man for the task. I'm flattered that he said yes to us when he had already turned down Nottingham Forest and Leicester City and I believe it is a decision he will be glad he made.' **(Robert Chase appoints a new manager, June 1995)**

'We pay Martin O'Neill a lot of money to manage the football department and the last thing he wants is me interfering.' **(Robert Chase, 1995)**

'I am not prepared to throw in the towel just because things are a bit rough at the moment.' **(Robert Chase, April 1996, three weeks before resigning as chairman)**

'I'm very excited. It's every supporter's dream to have some say in the club and I'm very interested to learn.' **(Delia Smith joins the board, November 1996)**

'When I do something in my life I never go into it without a great deal of enthusiasm – watch this space.' **(Delia Smith joins the City board, 1996)**

'It's time to stop dreaming about past glories. We need to re-align ourselves to plan the best possible route to reach the summit of achievement in British football.' **(City director Michael Wynn Jones, June 1998)**

'Eighteen months ago I thought we had a dream team and we were on our way and it's awful to think we got it wrong.' **(Delia Smith on Bruce Rioch's resignation as manager, March 2000)**

'I went to see him on behalf of the board and he told me there was nothing else on the table. Bruce is an honourable man and I believe him. I could have sat there all night. It was quite clear to me that he had made his mind up.' **(City director Barry Skipper on Bruce Rioch's resignation as manager, March 2000)**

'There are certain people who wanted to destroy the manager. I would never have believed it was possible. It was wicked and shameful.' **(Delia Smith defends Bryan Hamilton, 2001)**

'Myself, Doug Livermore and Steve Foley are going to the board of directors and we want some straight answers.' **(Acting manager Nigel Worthington wants to know if he has the top job, New Year's Day 2001)**

'A manager spends his first year getting rid of the players he inherited from the last one, the second year trying to get hold of the players that he wants and the third year

trying to get them into a team that's in his own image.'
(Michael Wynn Jones, 2003)

'Winning promotion to the Premiership was the icing
on the cake. Winning the title is the icing on the icing.'
(Delia Smith, 2004)

'Geoffrey Watling was in my view the best chairman
Norwich City ever had. He always dealt with people in a
nice way if he wanted anything done without shouting the
orders and always thanked you afterwards. We travelled
to many matches together. He hardly ever missed an
away game and in all he did he never charged the club
a penny.' **(Former City secretary Bert Westwood,
2004)**

'Charlton Athletic is the ideal model for Norwich City. I
have letters from Charlton fans thanking me for saying
that.' **(Delia Smith, 2004)**

'Would I swap my office at Carrow Road for an office
anywhere else in football? Not a chance.' **(City chief
executive Neil Doncaster, 2006)**

'Other chairmen told me that they enjoyed us playing
in the Premiership because we had cracking games of
football but we were beatable.' **(City chairman Roger
Munby, 2006)**

'We and the board are deeply disappointed by the lack
of passion and commitment in the team's performance
on Saturday and wish to apologise particularly to the 776
loyal supporters who undertook the long and arduous
journey to Plymouth, but also to all our fans who have
given us such wonderful support. You deserve more. We
are determined to achieve success at Norwich City and to
that end we expect the situation to be rectified at our next
home game on Sunday, and our next away game.' **(Delia**

Smith and Michael Wynn Jones react to 3-1 defeat at Plymouth, 2006)**

'We should certainly not be where we are in the table at the moment. Our supporters do not deserve what they witnessed on Saturday. They are entitled to expect better performances.' **(Neil Doncaster, September 2007)**

'With hindsight, observations come to mind about the previous manager, and the one before that. Both had the technical ability and the integrity, but the appropriateness of the appointments for our club is another matter.' **(Chairman Roger Munby regrets appointing Peter Grant and Glenn Roeder)**

'Under your chairmanship and Neil Doncaster's executive leadership, the quality of our product has deteriorated every year since 2004, losses have continued to mount and debt piled up. The only honourable course open to you both is to resign forthwith without compensation and for the board to seek a new chief executive, appoint a new chairman and work with the current majority shareholders to get us out of this mess.' **(Joint letter from associate directors Nigel Bertram and Alan Bowkett to chairman Roger Munby, May 2009)**

'It is clear that for Norwich City to move forward there needs to be a fresh start. A new board of directors is an essential part of that process. We therefore believe it is in the best interests of the club for us to step down from our positions.' **(Joint statement by Roger Munby and Neil Doncaster, 12 May 2009)**

'Truly this is one of the most exciting days of my life and I am as proud and pleased as I could be.' **(Stephen Fry becomes a City director)**

'We had a shortlist this time round of five people and Chris was top. We had a German, two Italians and a Scotsman. I'll leave you to guess which one is which.' **(Chairman Alan Bowkett on the appointment of Chris Hughton as City manager, June 2012)**

'The reason we took longer than we wanted to take was because we did a review of the German market, the Italian market, Spanish market, the whole of the British Isles, to find the candidate who stood the best chance of getting us promotion as soon as possible.' **(Chairman Alan Bowkett confirms Neil Adams as manager, 2014)**

(15)

A Kick Up The Eighties

'I am very pleased and feel it is a great honour. I have been here a long time and it is the ultimate in my career at the club.' **(Graham Paddon becomes City captain, January 1981)**

'Martin will do so much for this club. To think we have got someone of his calibre is marvellous. He can do exactly the same job Martin Peters did for us when he came here. You can't say more than that.' **(Ken Brown signs Martin O'Neill, February 1981)**

'I'm really hoping this turns out to be a permanent transfer. I have plenty to prove. I don't want to go back to reserve team football. I'm sure I've made the right choice.' **(Goalkeeper Chris Woods arrives on loan from Queens Park Rangers, March 1981)**

'I was marking Joe Royle that day and he was really upset after the game. The feeling of relegation is the worst ever. The first thing you realise is that you won't be playing at Old Trafford and Anfield the next season.' **(Leicester centre-half John O'Neill on a 3-2 win at Norwich as both clubs go down, 1981)**

'Losing the game took away some of the enjoyment of the goal but for those couple of seconds before they scored again, that is as good as it gets.' **(Keith Bertschin scores in a 2-1 defeat by Sheffield Wednesday but City are promoted, 1982)**

'Promotion was, honestly, as exciting as European Cup success with Nottingham Forest.' **(Martin O'Neill, 1982)**

'The first time we went up I was still a youngster really at 22. When we went up again in 1982, I was captain and that was brilliant. We were on such a confidence-boosting run, winning game after game, and we really didn't feel we could ever get beaten. We won ten out of 11 games in the run-in.' **(Mick McGuire recalls his promotion double)**

'I've often thought about sitting down and writing a letter to Kenny but I've never got round to doing it.' **(John Bond on parting from his former assistant, Ken Brown)**

'When we lost the toss for the replay we went back to Goodison and there were more than 20,000 there, more than they were getting for a lot of their league games.' **(Dave Stringer recalls City's FA Youth Cup Final victory over Everton, 1983)**

'I really wish we had been able to resolve something down here last season and that I was still playing for Norwich. I can understand the crowd giving me some stick but I just hope they understand that there are two sides to every story.' **(Martin O'Neill scores Notts County's winner at Carrow Road, 1984)**

'Some Norwich games get more coverage in Norway than they do in this country.' **(City defender Aage Hareide, 1984)**

'I think it is Mr Brown's philosophy that a football team should have entertainment as a priority. Once they get the breaks then Norwich will really do something.' **(Goalkeeper Joe Corrigan, October 1984)**

'I was called out at 4am and when I got down to the ground, the place was blazing like hell. Of course I felt sorry but it was Saturday's game of football I was worried about.' **(Sir Arthur South reacts to the Main Stand fire, 1984)**

'I am very sad. Stands can be rebuilt, sentimental things cannot.' **(Geoffrey Watling's bust perishes in the Carrow Road fire, 1984)**

'I was very lucky to play with some great players at Norwich and Mick Channon was top of the tree.' **(Mark Barham)**

'Ken Brown pulled us all into the changing rooms at the end of the season and said, "The door's open if you want to go," but no one stood up. We all felt we needed to repair what we'd just done.' **(Mark Barham on City's shock relegation, 1985)**

'It was the board's intention to build a stand similar to that at West Bromwich Albion. In the event, the cost of reproducing that stand here at Norwich proved to be more than we could afford.' **(Sir Arthur South explains scaled-down plans for the new City Stand, July 1985)**

'It wasn't one of my best games but I'll always remember that I scored the goal that clinched us the Second Division championship.' **(Dale Gordon secures a 1-1 draw against Stoke, April 1986)**

'Although it has taken a year longer than I thought when I came here, I'm greatly looking forward to playing in the First Division.' **(David Williams celebrates promotion, 1986)**

'I was absolutely delighted because they came back after we went down and said they would back me. Right from the word go we were on an up.' **(Ken Brown recalls winning the Second Division title straight after relegation, 1986)**

'Coming to a football match within the City Stand is very much like going to the theatre – the only difference being that our stage is covered with grass.' **(City chairman Robert Chase, 1986)**

'Mel Machin was a superb coach and although we didn't always see eye to eye, he knew exactly what he wanted from us.' **(Mark Barham)**

'People are already saying we won't be there for long. No disrespects to Wimbledon but I think we are better equipped to stay near the top.' **(City skipper Steve Bruce on leading the First Division, October 1986)**

'I don't remember much about any saves, but I do remember tackling Remi Moses almost on the halfway line as United broke away from a corner. I don't think people expected to see that.' **(Goalkeeper Bryan Gunn recalls his third appearance for City, against Manchester United, 1986)**

'We've been chasing this one for a long time. We've seen the lad several times and I know he has been scoring regularly for Rangers and I'm confident he can do the same for us.' **(City boss Dave Stringer signs striker Robert Fleck for a club record £580,000, December 1987)**

'Look at old Stringer – been to Augusta once in his life.' **(Millwall manager John Docherty notices the City manager's new green club blazer, 1989)**

'Ian presents himself well to the public and projects the kind of image we want to be associated with the club.' **(Dave Stringer appoints Ian Butterworth as captain, 1989)**

'I think what I shall do after Christmas is learn some of the favourite Irish ballads and, if I'm picked, take my acoustic guitar out to Italy with me.' **(City midfielder Andy Townsend prepares for a World Cup call-up, 1989)**

'I wrote to Norwich City when Ken Brown was the manager because my auntie lived in Wymondham. I said I would stay with her if they would just give me a chance of a week's trial. I was only 13 at the time.' **(Striker Malcolm Allen, 1989, eight years after first trying to join City)**

'We could have been about 7-2 down in spite of being two up so early. Big Gunny played brilliantly, and Ian St John gave Terry Hurlock the man of the match, which was a disgrace.' **(Robert Fleck on the televised 3-2 win at Millwall, 1989)**

(16)

It's A Man's Game

'It was a stupid incident really…anyway [Tommy] Robson knocked me into the back of the net. I completely lost my rag, put the ball under one arm and laid him out with the other. He was out cold for a couple of minutes and had to have six stitches over his eye. He's a nice bloke as well.' **(Kevin Keelan becomes the first City goalkeeper to be sent off, against Northampton, 1965)**

'It was not a very common injury and not many people knew what it was. When the club doctor said it was cruciate ligaments it could have been toothache as far as I was concerned. They didn't operate in those days. You were finished as a footballer and that was it.' **(Full-back Phil Kelly recalls his career-ending injury, 1965)**

'I remember playing against Bill Baxter and it was nothing to do with him being Scottish and me being Welsh but I didn't like the way he played. We had a real battle but I can guarantee that I won.' **(Centre-forward Laurie Sheffield on scoring in a 2-0 win at Ipswich, 1967)**

'Mick Mills was playing full-back for Ipswich and he brought me down from behind and I had to go off with an ankle injury. Mick was a fine player because, of course, he went on to play for England but I knew I'd got him for pace that day.' **(Charlie Crickmore on a bruising derby against Ipswich, 1968)**

'I watched as one player wearily took off his mud-caked boots and rolled down his socks. His shinbones were uneven as xylophones, due to the close attentions of opposing players who over the years had kicked lumps out of him. Blood was trickling over his feet. He looked at me, shrugged his shoulders, and dragged himself off to the bath.' **(Bruce Robinson, *Passing Seasons*)**

'I remember Roger Hynd, the Birmingham captain, who was a massive fellow everyone was scared of, trying to put Kevin Keelan into the back of the net. When Hynd got up off the floor, he had six stud marks on his face. I was only 19 and that frightened me a bit.' **(Centre-half Steve Govier on a promotion clash, 1971)**

'When I was first taught to play, the first tackle was always from behind, straight through the man. If he looked behind him next time you knew you'd done your job and you'd have no problems.' **(Steve Govier)**

'They had to cut a hole and put a tube into the lung and I had to carry this big demijohn full of water around for three or four days until my lung came back to its normal size. It was an experience I'll never forget.' **(Duncan Forbes suffers a punctured lung at Highbury, 1972)**

'I spent a week in the Royal Northern Hospital, Holloway Road, and it was quite a dour place. I remember going in there after the Arsenal game and somebody next to me was coughing and spluttering. When I woke up the next morning he was gone. He had died in the night.' **(Duncan Forbes)**

'I just can't put into words how I felt – how low, how depressed. Every player is afraid to be put on the sidelines for a long time.' **(Striker Peter Silvester, after two years out injured, 1973)**

'I'm not having it set right away. When they suggested I had the nose done immediately, I pointed out that we were at Arsenal on Tuesday.' **(Duncan Forbes breaks his nose against Aston Villa, August 1975)**

'As centre-halves go, I'm not very big. Under six feet tall, and I weigh less than 12 stone. So most of the centre-forwards are bigger, heavier and stronger than me. Stopping them usually takes more out of me than them.' **(Duncan Forbes, 1975)**

'There have been many criticisms of his style, usually listed under the headings of Iron Man, Yellow Peril and Raw Meat. However, he has soaked them up with a big smile and the proud boast that he has never hurt a fellow professional or been sent off.' **(Keith Skipper on Duncan Forbes, September 1976)**

'I knew even before I hit the ground that the leg was broken. I had no doubt at all. It was a frightening moment.' **(City midfielder Graham Paddon, injured at Sunderland, 1976)**

'It was going quite well when I first signed but I got a hamstring injury and was out for about ten weeks. I was made to train when I should have rested it, and ended up having cortisone injections and all sorts of treatment. I got the injury problems and had a bust-up with the gaffer.' **(Viv Busby on his 12 months with City)**

'I think police should have more instant power. I'm talking in terms of physical retaliation against the louts with police dogs if necessary.' **(Duncan Forbes reacts to rioting by Manchester United fans at Carrow Road, April 1977)**

'I scored four goals in the first seven games and then against Birmingham I ran through and my Achilles went. It was a sharp pain and quite a bad tear. They decided to immobilise the Achilles and rest it. I didn't have the operation and in hindsight I should have had it done. I think John Bond looked at me – I was 33 – and didn't want to wait for me to recover from an operation.' **(Martin Chivers suffers a major injury blow, 1978)**

'I remember chasing Trevor Cherry, who was playing right-back. He tried to play one up the line and I just caught him. It took about 45 seconds before I went up in the air and Cherry said, "That's a little warning son, if you catch me again." It was a harsh introduction.' **(Greg Downs recalls facing Leeds, 1978)**

'Every time I got a run in the team I seemed to get cartilage or ligament problems. I had four knee operations but they didn't have the sports science to deal with it that they have now.' **(Doug Evans)**

'I still partake occasionally with the gloves and I believe it's good for me still because I work the aggression out of my system.' **(Striker and ex-boxer Justin Fashanu, 1979)**

'My landlord Mick Hunter was an army sprint champion in the Parachute Regiment and he has had me pulling a tractor tyre to sharpen me up over ten yards.' **(Midfielder Peter Mendham, 1981)**

'He looks as if he's just been ten rounds with Muhammad Ali.' **(Steve Walford on fellow defender Dave Watson's facial injury after a clash with Everton's Graeme Sharp, 1982)**

'I hadn't been booked and all that happened was Speedie grabbed my arm and I tried to swing him off. My hand caught him but it wasn't hard enough to knock my little boy over and he is only two. It's the first time in my career that I have been sent off.' **(Shaun Elliott, sent off at Coventry, 1988)**

'I just wasn't as fit as I'd hoped to be. I seemed to be permanently injured – knees, ribs, Achilles. Then Ken Brown signed Ian Butterworth, who was much younger, so there was only going to be one outcome.' **(Shaun Elliott)**

'Some of the lads were spat upon as they went down the tunnel after the match. When the trouble started there were Arsenal players racing 30 to 40 yards to join in. I think I'd better take my boxing gloves out for the next game.' **(City skipper Ian Butterworth on the Highbury 'brawl', November 1989)**

'At grounds like Highbury the crowd are screaming every time something happens in the box. And 35,000 shouting is a bit different to 16,000 at Carrow Road. All through the game they were on the referee's back. I realise referees have a difficult job but they have to learn to withstand that kind of pressure.' **(Ian Butterworth on the Highbury 'brawl', 1989)**

'A lot has been made of a little scuffle which lasted no more than ten seconds. Most of us were just trying to calm the situation down. The referee didn't feel it warranted any bookings and I saw no punches. The press has just blown the whole thing out of proportion.' **(Bryan Gunn on the Highbury 'brawl', 1989)**

'You just don't expect the club to be involved in things like that. It used to have such a good reputation in the past that it makes it more of a shock now. The whole country knows Norwich are a good footballing side. They are never dirty.' **(David Fullman, Lord Mayor of Norwich, on the Highbury 'brawl', November 1989)**

'They're hooligans. If the fans had not been segregated then there would have been a riot. Of that there is no doubt. If those scenes had happened in the crowd there is no doubt people would have been arrested and sent to prison.' **(Alan Eastwood, chairman of the Police Federation, on the Highbury 'brawl', 1989)**

'At least two of the players on the Norwich team would have found it difficult to defend any actions the FA might have brought on the basis of what we have seen this afternoon.' **(FA chief executive Graham Kelly announces a £50,000 fine for Norwich City, November 1989)**

'If it gives me a chance of making it to the semi-finals, I will sleep in it.' **(Robert Fleck hopes an oxygen chamber will help cure two broken ribs, March 1992)**

'Even with a gammy leg I'm better off than a lot of people. I've got rid of the chauffeur. Hopefully in a couple of weeks I'll be able to get rid of the crutches as well.' **(Winger Matthew Rush, injured in training after one first-team appearance, 1995)**

'I started to walk off and all of a sudden the mob came on. It was pretty frightening. They all wanted a fight.' **(Robert Fleck survives a pitch invasion at Ipswich, 1996)**

'The danger is some people think if you play good football that somehow means you don't compete, but if you look at the best teams in any league they all tackle and compete as well.' **(Mike Walker, 1996)**

'I'm quite glad our lads stood up and were counted. They showed a reaction and I haven't been getting that for a while.' **(Mike Walker after the 21-man brawl against Crystal Palace, December 1996)**

'I think it's still going to have to be an incredibly bad tackle from behind for the referee to send a player off straightaway. I really hope there aren't too many red or yellow cards.' **(Craig Fleming anticipates a change in the law, 1998)**

'If I'd been standing on my left leg it would have snapped, but I was standing on my right leg and that's what made the difference.' **(Craig Bellamy on surviving Kevin Muscat's horror tackle at Wolves, 1998)**

'I was probably the closest player to the incident and saw what Muscat did to Bellamy and I can remember him sitting next to me on the team bus with a hole in his knee.' **(Neil Adams remembers Molineux, 1998)**

'When you're injured, all sorts of things go through your mind. It's the biggest test I've had, going from a high when you're scoring to feeling devastated when you're out of the team.' **(Craig Bellamy, April 1999)**

'Jacko was in the dressing room, whingeing as usual. I think he's just worried about his good looks.' **(Goalkeeper Robert Green marks his City debut by breaking skipper Matt Jackson's nose in a collision, 1999)**

'There are no prima donnas here. We don't have any tantrums. There's no one who is going to refuse to come back, to go on strike.' **(Manager Bruce Rioch, 1999)**

'All I thought about is the calibre of player that has come back from this injury – Del Piero, Shearer, Robbie Fowler.' **(Craig Bellamy prepares for nine months on the sidelines with a knee injury, July 1999)**

'I only spat down at the pitch, not in the air and certainly not towards the Rangers supporters. That would not have been right. But they all went crazy.' **(Pape Diop denies provoking Queens Park Rangers fans, December 1999)**

'When you have a knee injury like that, one of the first things you have to do is learn to run again without a limp.' **(Zema Abbey, 2002)**

'Do I miss it? The whole time. I miss the start of the season, the end of the season, the middle of the season.' **(Darren Eadie, forced to retire through injury, 2003)**

'The truth is that Dean Ashton has a groin injury – and we have the medical scans to prove it, which show the damage in the groin area.' **(Nigel Worthington insists Dean Ashton was injured for City's FA Cup tie against West Ham just before he joined the Hammers, January 2006)**

'The injury was a major blow from a psychological point of view. Was Robert ready then? We shall never know. If he is called upon I am sure he will do a very good job for England.' **(Nigel Worthington on Robert Green's pre-World Cup groin injury)**

'I've seen it many times and been involved in it a few times myself. When you get a small group of people in a close-knit scenario for nine to ten months a season, these sort of spats are going to happen. It finished up as handbags. They've had a clout at each other, now let's get on with it.' **(Nigel Worthington on a training ground bust-up between Dickson Etuhu and Youssef Safri, September 2006)**

'If it was a head-butt, he'd still be lying there.' **(Manager Peter Grant disputes Dion Dublin's red card for a challenge on Charlton's Danny Mills, September 2007)**

'Norwich are too nice. Teams come to Norwich looking forward to the game. The players, and this includes me, have got to get nasty. Teams ought to expect 90 minutes of hell when they come to Norwich.' **(Dion Dublin, 2007)**

'I think when you look at the great players around the world, they've all got an edge to them. They're all nice guys when they need to be nice and most of them nasty, ruthless people on the football field, whatever position they play.' **(Manager Glenn Roeder, November 2007)**

'I was delighted to sign for Norwich because I thought it was a great move for me. I was buzzing, it was the move I wanted, but I got a bad injury in my first game and then never really got my fitness back.' **(Luke Chadwick, 2009)**

'The best way of summing Jimmy up as a footballer is that he would run through brick walls for you.' **(Ken Brown pays tribute to late City winger Jimmy Neighbour, April 2009)**

'I don't really know what you've got to do for a tackle. I don't think it was even a tackle in the sense I was already favourite to win the ball and I was merely guiding it on to Simon Lappin. The lad has run in from behind, right into me, and somehow the referee has decided to send me off.' **(Darel Russell gets the eighth red card of his career for a 'dangerous challenge' on Southampton's Morgan Schneiderlin, February 2010)**

'Jason Shackell will be devastated because his two front teeth are gone, so we're out on the pitch looking for them to see if we can put them back in.' **(Barnsley boss Mark Robins sympathises with the ex-City defender, February 2011)**

'James is away to see the plastic surgeon at the minute so it's a bad one. It's gone right through the lip. We just can't stitch it up.' **(Paul Lambert gives a medical update on striker James Vaughan, elbowed by West Bromwich Albion defender Gabriel Tamas, 2011)**

'I suppose it was sod's law that it had to be Dave. It happened on only the second day of training when I dived to stop one of his shots. We got the glove off immediately and the finger was already black so we knew it wasn't good.' **(Goalkeeper John Ruddy misses Euro 2012 with a broken finger inflicted by goalkeeping coach Dave Watson)**

'Every game is a battle. You don't go out there in the Premier League and get an easy game – never. You need to bite and scratch, do everything you possibly can as an individual to try to do better than your opponent.' **(Robert Snodgrass, 2013)**

'When I go in to a tackle I want to win it but I never go out with the intention of hurting anyone. When I signed for Norwich Paul Lambert said I had a nasty side to my game and that's true. But I'm not dirty.' **(City midfielder Bradley Johnson responds to criticism from Arsenal, 2013)**

(17)

Have They Got News For You

'The Cits are dead but the Canaries are very much alive.' **(Local newspaper headline captures a new nickname, and a change of colours to yellow and green, 1907)**

'The gate, of course, was greatly affected by the international situation. Instead of the 25,000 which the Ipswich officials confidently said would have been present had times been normal, the attendance was 10,792.' **(*Eastern Daily Press* report on the first Ipswich v Norwich derby, on the eve of war, 2 September 1939)**

'I remember so vividly after that unlucky semi-final defeat by Luton at Birmingham, Archie Macaulay turning to me and saying, "What are you looking so fed up about?" The utter disappointment I felt must have shown through my mask of impartiality. I felt thoroughly deflated. This was the end of the road. For Norwich City. And for my story…I believed in Norwich City as I have never believed in a team before.' **(John Bromley, *Canary Crusade*, 1959)**

'Archie Macaulay, the man who built the new Norwich City, talked ME into believing that a miracle was about to be performed. It was a masterpiece of salesmanship. But more important, of course, was the fact that Macaulay had already sold the idea of success to his team. That was the whole secret of Norwich City's fantastic assault on the FA Cup.' **(Ian Wooldridge, *Canary Crusade*, 1959)**

'Third Division clubs have had a good run in the cup, and before now have even reached the semi-final. But somehow they have always looked Third Division teams. The essential quality of Norwich City's performance lies in the fact that they were a "class" side: indeed, there were occasions when some of their opponents from higher levels deserved the label of "cloggers" far more than Norwich.' **(John Arlott, 1959)**

'Stanley Matthews was back at Stoke and all the photographers went down the end Stoke were attacking and I was alone at the other end. I got six goals that day and they got none.' **(*Eastern Daily Press* photographer Dick Jeeves recalls City's 6-0 home win over Stoke, 1963)**

'City have been accused often enough of thinking big, talking big but not acting big. They've acted big here, bigger than any Norwich City regime until the present one could have even dreamed of.' **(Ted Bell on the £35,000 signing of centre-forward Ron Davies, September 1963)**

'Derby have achieved their target and won promotion. City look 100 years away from it.' **(Dick Scales, *Eastern Evening News*, April 1969)**

'The facilities were less than sophisticated. The gantry at Carrow Road was behind the goal, which made it a test of observation. The first match I did was a 3-1 win against Blackpool. It was quite a test. There was no slow motion replay, you had to fit the slow motion in after you edited.' **(Gerry Harrison, *Match of the Week* commentator)**

'Hot Cross Bone Day!' **(*Pink Un* headline as David Cross and Jim Bone score on Easter Saturday, 1972)**

'Saunders has traded the goal flair of the Scottish international for the midfield drive and experience of the Blade who doesn't use a razor.' **(Keith Skipper on the Jim Bone-Trevor Hockey swap deal, *Pink Un*, February 1973)**

'This year I've seen them four or five times, and when I'm in New York I always look first for their result in the *New York Times*.' **(David Frost on following City, 1973)**

'Mr South's attacking football pledge on succeeding Geoffrey Watling as chairman wasn't greeted kindly by a manager who considered it his job to formulate any policy on the playing side.' **(Keith Skipper, *EDP*, November 1973)**

'The home of Liverpool has become football's Coliseum, with the opposition providing no more than fodder for the home team. Yet on Saturday the Christians slaughtered the lions. Norwich City began by having the temerity to warm up at the Kop end, and went on not only to beat Liverpool but also to make them look merely an average side.' **(Mick Dennis, *Eastern Evening News*, on City's 3-1 win at Anfield, November 1975)**

'Not since the days of 1959 can Carrow Road have generated such excitement. This was an afternoon when Norwich and Liverpool, with an unrelenting display of attacking football, richly illustrated the healthy state of the English game at club level.' **(Malcolm Robertson describes City's 5-3 home defeat by Liverpool, 1980)**

'Granville's goal was open all hours.' **(Bill Walker, *Eastern Evening News*, on City's 6-1 win over Millwall, December 1985)**

'Trust Norwich City to get it just right. A lot of clubs could learn a thing or two about the way you go about things. The more I see of this club, the more I am impressed.' **(BBC commentator Tony Gubba, 1987)**

'There's a line in Norwich's famous old club song, "On the Ball, City", which says, "Hurrah! We've scored a goal." Well, it's double hurrah now because they've scored two.' **(Martin Tyler, Sky TV commentator, Bayern Munich v City, 1993)**

'It's a tremendous victory and a wonderful scalp for Norwich. Probably the best moment in their history, I would think.' **(Desmond Lynam, BBC, after City knock out Bayern, 1993)**

'We certainly made a big production of it, there's no doubt about that, and when Norwich were knocked out we were very disappointed.' **(John Motson on the BBC's coverage of City in Europe)**

'He's got a head like an old threepenny bit.' **(Ian St John describes Norwich striker Robert Fleck, 1995)**

'As Sunderland celebrate their return to the top flight and Dean Windass bangs another one in for Aberdeen, let us acknowledge that City chairman and master mathematician Robert Chase has been spot on. Yes, 81 points would indeed have guaranteed automatic promotion.' **(Trevor Burton, *Eastern Daily Press*, April 1996)**

'I still think it has a lot of character, and it feels very Norwich to me. But the disappointing thing about Carrow

Road is where they have added the corners to the City Stand. Clearly they were an afterthought.' **(Simon Inglis, stadium expert and author, 1996)**

'After all the bile and derision that has seeped its way up the A140 since Bryan Gunn's misfortunes in last year's Portman Road clash and the general, ill-mannered hysteria in which Ian Crook's transfer saga was cast, the fact that Town returned south last night with cheeks burning from a thorough spanking has a feelgood factor the Tories would die for.' **(Rick Waghorn, *Evening News*, City 3 Ipswich 1, 1996)**

'I was offered a job with Radio Ipswich but I wouldn't work for that bunch of losers.' **(Alan Partridge, Radio Norwich)**

'Dunces with Wolves.' **(*Pink Un* headline after 5-0 defeat at Molineux, 1998)**

'The worst that comes to mind was during a very exciting game against Liverpool when I said, "And the referee is about to blow his watch." No one has ever let me forget that one.' **(BBC Radio Norfolk commentator Roy Waller)**

'The half-time rendition of "Nessun Dorma" at the West Brom game was rudely interrupted by a safety message. The soloist was just getting into his stride when the music cut out and a voiced boomed out, "Mr Carrow has left the stadium."' **(*Evening News* columnist, October 2001)**

'Listen to Nigel Worthington and it's a tale of woe, just like the BBC announcer who comes on when your TV picture disappears. He says it is due to circumstances beyond his control and work is going on behind the scenes to rectify it as soon as possible.' **(Richard Balls, columnist, September 2006)**

'What I can confirm is that Norwich will get the usual *Soccer Saturday* service – perhaps even better. Don't forget, we are in the same division now.' **(Sky Sports presenter and Hartlepool fan Jeff Stelling, 2009)**

'I will admit to sneaking a Norwich City tie on to the set one day. I wore it the entire four-hour shift. The tie was given to me by Jeremy Goss and I promised I would somehow get it on the telly.' **(Sky TV presenter Simon Thomas, 2010)**

'For once, there was a strange solidarity between the two sets of fans. The Yellow and Green Army chanted, "You're getting sacked in the morning," to Keane – Town's angry followers joined in.' **(Chris Lakey, *Eastern Daily Press*, on the 4-1 derby win over Ipswich, November 2010)**

'This was an iconic afternoon when all the planets seem to align perfectly, wrapped around the hugely impressive Neil, who meticulously plotted the downfall of a Middlesbrough foe that had inflicted two previous league defeats on the Canaries.' **(Paddy Davitt, *Eastern Daily Press*, on City's Championship play-off final victory, May 2015)**

Into The Limelight

(18)

'To the young boys in the team it must all seem to be happening in a little bit of a blur. You can't take it in at the time. Looking back, I played against people like Bobby Moore and Gordon Banks, but just didn't take it in.' **(Midfielder Max Briggs)**

'I remember playing United at Old Trafford in our second season up and getting a 0-0 draw. It was George Best's first game back after one of those spells when he fell out with the club. He hadn't played for three months but he was mesmerising, the way he played – a great player.' **(Supersub Trevor Howard on facing a legend, 1973)**

'The 70s was a great time to go to America but I used to look at some of those players like Pele, Eusebio and Beckenbauer and think, "What am I doing here?"' **(Ex-City goalkeeper Mervyn Cawston on life with Chicago Sting)**

'It was a blue arm which went up as we jumped – and it belonged to Joe Jordan. I had no idea the referee thought I'd handled. I didn't know until after the game, and then I was really sick.' **(David Jones pleads not guilty to conceding the penalty in a Wales v Scotland World Cup qualifier, 1977)**

'Teams will now be trying to knock us down for we have matched the best in the table and anyone who can take anything off Norwich will be considered to have done well.' **(Skipper Martin Peters after topping the First Division, 1979)**

'I was originally one of the substitutes but the match was fogged off. Keegan had a contract with Hamburg that meant he had to be back on Thursday before a weekend game, so I took his place. Glenn Hoddle and I made our debuts in the same match, which was absolutely fantastic.' **(Kevin Reeves makes his England debut against Bulgaria, 1979)**

'I thought we'd applaud them on so they wouldn't feel so bad about applauding us off after we'd beaten them. We came here to win and let them do the applauding.' **(Ken Brown on City's 2-0 win at newly-crowned champions Liverpool, April 1983)**

'I am sure if ET had landed he would have thought that the boys in yellow and green were the league champions.' **(Dave Watson on the 2-0 victory at Liverpool, 1983)**

'We were in Norway on our end-of-season tour. Ken Brown was on the other end of the phone and said, "Great news. Get your bags packed and get back to England because you've been picked for the squad for the England-Scotland game and you're going out to Australia." I said, "That's just brilliant, boss," and put the phone down and went back to sleep. I thought it was a wind-up.' **(Mark Barham is picked for England, 1983)**

'A couple of days before the Brazil game, Graham Roberts was rushed into hospital with appendicitis and had an operation, so that meant I was in for my debut. Before the game I remember Bobby Robson saying, "How are you feeling?" and I said I was nervous, but he said, "Think how your mum and dad must be feeling watching on TV."' **(Dave Watson recalls his first England cap in a 2-0 win in Rio, 1984)**

'You're daft if you're not ambitious and I would be telling lies if I said I wasn't hoping for the job.' **(Mike Walker is appointed City manager, 1992)**

'The figures show we are the best team in the country. We keep being told about these hard games we're facing, but they're only as hard as you make them.' **(Mike Walker after a 3-2 Premier League win at Aston Villa, November 1992)**

'We deserve to be in third place overall and I would have been very disappointed if we hadn't achieved it. We have entertained right to the end and finished as we have gone on all season, scoring plenty of goals and conceding plenty.' **(Mike Walker, May 1993)**

'We have achieved something which people will say isn't bad in your first season, but we've got to try to improve on that. That's the goal. We've got to try to win the Premier League next year.' **(Mike Walker, May 1993)**

'When I came to Norwich, even before we kicked a ball, we were favourites for relegation. In the end we were pushing for the league title until the last seven or eight games.' **(Gary Megson)**

'They didn't like to be beaten, no doubt about it. They were stung by it because they got a lot of flak from their own media about getting beaten by what they thought was a second-rate English team, this unknown club from East Anglia.' **(Ian Butterworth on the UEFA Cup win over Bayern Munich, 1993)**

'European games were not 100mph like the Premier League so people that could play and pass were going to excel – people with a bit of intelligence. And we had a team more or less like that.' **(Mike Walker on City's UEFA Cup experience)**

'It was great to be able to talk to Billy Wright and Ferenc Puskas. There was a disco afterwards and it would have been nice to have stayed and enjoyed the social side. But of course I had to get Gunny back to Norwich because of another TV date – the game against Leeds next day. The job takes priority.' **(Mike Walker and goalkeeper Bryan Gunn are guests at the BBC Sports Personality of the Year ceremony, 1993)**

'Mike Walker let John Deehan take training but he made the decisions in the office and was calm and in control all the time. He was successful right from the word go, so that made it easier for him.' **(Gary Megson, January 1994)**

'The last game in front of the Kop was a bit special. On the day we were only there as bit-part players and yet we won 1-0. We really played some fantastic stuff that day.' **(Ian Crook remembers the 1994 victory at Anfield)**

'The best game for me was winning against Arsenal 2-1 in the last game of the season away from home in 1987. One of the newspapers described us as a gathering of First Division rejects and Third and Fourth Division misfits. For us to finish fifth was unbelievable.' **(Ian Crook)**

'You do get that adrenalin rush from TV. The crowd sense it, too, when they turn up and see those big broadcasting units outside the stadium. You felt as players there was the opportunity to perform on the big stage and there might just be somebody watching. It was an added incentive. We thrived on the opportunity, we found that extra five or ten per cent. At Norwich we had so many TV games that quite a few players became big transfer targets as a result.' **(Dale Gordon on City's live TV dates)**

'We always got a lot of pleasure out of beating Manchester United. We wanted to show them how good we were.' **(Robert Fleck recalls five straight wins over Alex Ferguson's men)**

'This is such an important time for me with the England game coming up and to be left out of the action with my club leaves me very, very bitter. If you're not playing for your own team, you aren't going to be called up for England.' **(Dale Gordon, dropped at Liverpool, April 1991)**

'Because I was born outside the UK but carry a UK passport, I'm entitled to play for any of the four home countries. Look at me, supposedly Mr Very Average, being watched by the manager of a national team.' **(City midfielder Jeremy Goss is watched by Wales, April 1991)**

'I just caught it so sweetly. You don't need to hit these balls very hard and as soon as I hit it I knew it was going in.' **(Jeremy Goss describes his goal against Bayern Munich in the Olympic Stadium, Munich, 1993)**

'I reacted instinctively, throwing myself towards Valencia and in the general direction of the ball, which smashed into my goolies and rebounded back to Kreuzer who thumped it over the bar. It doesn't matter how you stop them, just as long as you keep them out.' **(Bryan Gunn on his save against Bayern Munich's Adolfo Valencia, 1993)**

'I ended up in front of where the players' wives and girlfriends were sitting, near where the Snakepit is now, and my mum came running down to meet me. She grabbed hold of me and I'm hugging my mum! I just couldn't believe it because we certainly hadn't planned to meet like that.' **(Jeremy Goss celebrates his goal in the second leg against Bayern Munich, 1993)**

'The feeling among the players afterwards was that we hadn't disgraced ourselves. We'd put on a good show, put Norwich on the map and gained a lot of good publicity for the club by playing good attractive open football. We surprised a lot of people – television commentators and ordinary fans around the country.' **(Jeremy Goss on City's UEFA Cup run, 1993)**

'It was disappointing not to be included in the squad but it's given me the opportunity to book my holidays in Cyprus.' **(Scotland goalkeeper Bryan Gunn misses out on Euro 96)**

'Buffon was in goal and he went on to be regarded as the best goalkeeper in the world. It was quite a bizarre goal because he came out to try to shepherd the ball out for a goal kick. I chased it down and forced him into touch, off the pitch, and I managed to turn and put the ball in from a tight angle.' **(Darren Eadie recalls his goal for England Under-21s against Italy, 1997)**

'I think it's probably fair to say that Justin was a more talented player than John and people would have expected him to have a better career and probably go on to play for England.' **(Former City chief scout Ronnie Brooks on the Fashanu brothers, 1998)**

'I went to the World Cup with my country and played a couple of games and that's got to be the pinnacle of anyone's career. But to be the manager of Norwich City in a play-off final in Cardiff, with that kind of atmosphere, that kind of support, is one of the best days I've had in football.' **(Nigel Worthington, 2002)**

'It's not "I", it's "we" at this football club. It's teamwork. We've all worked very, very hard together.' **(Nigel Worthington celebrates winning the First Division title, May 2004)**

'I don't say, "Right, I'm going to play for England," but as long as I work as hard as I can and improve as much as I can, then anything is possible.' **(Dean Ashton, January 2005, three years before winning his one England cap)**

'I was playing against Gillingham one minute in the Johnstone's Paint Trophy and then the next minute I was on a plane on the way to Japan. Tokyo was a long way to go but it was really worth it with me getting my first cap.' **(City midfielder Stephen Hughes makes his Scotland debut, October 2009)**

'Grant has my full admiration, not only for what he has done at this football club, but with other teams as well. However, if I was to give an England cap to every player who had my admiration then I am afraid we would need around 420 places, and we do not have quite that many.' **(England manager Roy Hodgson explains his failure to select Grant Holt, November 2012)**

19

On The Outside Looking In

'I have played in some of the world's greatest stadiums but I have never experienced an atmosphere like that. The crowd is worth a goal start for Norwich.' **(Tottenham's Danny Blanchflower, 1959)**

'You have to be a hard case not to feel sorry for a side who suffered as they did when the fog came down. Now they've made it, and I hope they win the cup at Wembley.' **(Chelsea manager Dave Sexton, January 1973)**

'It was the best match I've ever played in and Justin Fashanu's goal must be the finest of the season.' **(Liverpool defender Phil Thompson on their 5-3 win at Norwich, February 1980)**

'If anyone had to beat us I'm glad it was Norwich for I hope they stay up as it would be good for East Anglian football.' **(Ipswich boss Bobby Robson after derby defeat ended his team's title hopes, Easter Monday 1981)**

'I think Martin lasted longer as a player than Moore and Hurst because he was a midfield player and experience can get you by more in midfield than at the back or in attack.' **(Trevor Brooking on Martin Peters, 1981)**

'You don't tiptoe through the tulips and win games of football. Norwich wanted to win and deserved to. We deserved what we got.' **(Liverpool manager Bob Paisley after 2-0 home defeat by Norwich, April 1983)**

'Happy with the draw? I was until I saw Norwich on the telly. They frightened me to death.' **(Derby manager Peter Taylor looks ahead to the FA Cup fifth round tie, 1984)**

'This is a rare occasion. I'm not often happy with a draw.' **(Alex Ferguson collects his first point as Manchester United manager in a 0-0 draw at Norwich, November 1986)**

'Ian Crook has been the steal of the season.' **(England manager Bobby Robson before giving Crook a B international cap, 1987)**

'Dean was complaining of double vision in the first half. I think he could see two goals and that's why he managed to hit one of them.' **(QPR boss Jim Smith hails Dean Coney's stunning goal in a 3-0 win against City, 1988)**

'They tell me Princess Anne's getting divorced. Do you want me to comment on that as well?' **(Liverpool manager Kenny Dalglish is asked about his reported interest in City's Robert Fleck, 1990)**

'Dave Stringer is doing a magnificent job at Carrow Road, a fact which doesn't surprise me in the least because back in my days as manager of Cambridge, he was the best signing I made and an excellent skipper.' **(Aston Villa manager Ron Atkinson, 1992)**

'It seemed as if Norwich played with 15 players at first because they made things so difficult for us.' **(Dennis Bergkamp, Inter Milan, 1993)**

'I thought I was going to Norwich. I waved bye bye to the Hull fans twice, for my last game.' **(Hull's Dean Windass joins Aberdeen instead of City, 1995)**

'I wish every other chairman in the country the best of British luck in dealing with Mr Chase because they are going to need it.' **(Hull chairman Martin Fish, December 1995)**

'If Norwich don't make a quick return to the Premiership, the blame will be as much in the boardroom as in the dressing room, if not more so.' **(Alan Hansen, 1996, eight years before City managed to return)**

'We looked abroad but I wanted a man who eats fish and chips and has a normal personality.' **(Sheffield Wednesday manager David Pleat signs City centre-half Jon Newsome, 1996)**

'Norwich must be the quickest team in the league. Darren Eadie should be playing for England, let alone Norwich. He's so quick he's unbelievable.' **(Tranmere player-boss John Aldridge, 1996)**

'I liken him to Michael Owen. In training on Friday he was putting the ball into the net just like Jimmy Greaves.' **(Wales manager Bobby Gould assesses Craig Bellamy)**

'Should've picked Roberts. Plays for Norwich. Used to be Wolves. Good in the air.' **(*EastEnders* character Matthew Rose watches Italy v Wales, 1999)**

'Andy comes to us from our East Anglian neighbours Norwich City. But it doesn't matter where you come from. When you pull on the blue and white shirt of Ipswich Town you are a Town player and that's all that matters.' **(Ipswich chairman David Sheepshanks welcomes goalkeeper Andy Marshall on a free transfer from Norwich, 2001)**

'If they go up, they'll come straight down. They need at least 15 new players. I would rather see any team go up other than Norwich. It should have been all over in the first half.' **(Ipswich defender Fabian Wilnis reacts badly to a 3-1 defeat at Norwich, March 2004)**

'It's great to see you again, Keith. I just hope you haven't brought that flaming Deehan with you.' **(Ex-Watford goalkeeper Steve Sherwood, who conceded ten goals from City's John Deehan in four seasons, meets Keith Bertschin on a scouting mission)**

'I won't deny I flipped my fingers in his direction, but only because I was so disgusted and frustrated at being humiliated by a fellow manager. I held out my hand for six or seven seconds but he turned his back.' **(Sheffield United manager Neil Warnock accuses Nigel Worthington of refusing a handshake, 2006)**

'Should Norwich City wish to buy our player I suggest Glenn should just pick up the phone and call me.' **(Birmingham managing director Karren Brady invites Glenn Roeder to make her an offer for centre-half Martin Taylor, 2007)**

'I scored a lot of goals for them and, to be honest, the response I've had from Ipswich fans since I signed for Norwich, everyone I have met has been totally positive and really happy for me. People leave football clubs, it's just football. There's no point in getting angry about it or worked up.' **(City loan striker Alan Lee prepares to visit former club Ipswich, April 2009)**

'Their board were pilloried for sacking Bryan Gunn after one league match but I said at the time that bringing in Paul Lambert so quickly and so ruthlessly might prove to be a shrewd move.' **(Ex-Leeds star Peter Lorimer, October 2009)**

'It was funny. I remember one of the old guys on the board asking me, "Do you think your style of football would go down well with the Norwich fans?" and I just took a deep breath, looked around the table and said, "What do you mean, winning?"' **(Neil Warnock, 2010)**

'Although I was born and bred in Norwich, I'm now a Leeds fan because of the great times I had there as a player. When I left Norwich it was not on great terms.' **(Danny Mills, 2010)**

'It's the first time as a manager I've lost by six goals. I was praying for a plague of locusts or anything to help.' **(Scunthorpe manager Alan Knill on his side's 6-0 defeat at Norwich, April 2011)**

'I think Delia is a wonderful woman and Norwich is a great club.' **(Neil Warnock, 2011)**

'It was evident from the early stages that the Canaries were favourites for this title.' **(Competition spokesman as City win the Premier League Shirts Cup for best kit, 2011)**

'They've got their own little empire down there. It's just like when I was at Aberdeen. It feels like you're cut off from everywhere. Nonetheless they're being very successful with it.' **(Sir Alex Ferguson on Norwich, February 2012)**

20

The Wilderness Years

'It just needs one brick to be knocked out of the wall by someone being sold, or leaving as Mike Walker did, and very quickly an outstanding side can become mediocre.' **(Efan Ekoku recalls City's fall from grace after Europe)**

'I now feel a lot more in control of my own destiny. Last season there were too many skeletons rattling in the background.' **(John Deehan, January 1995)**

'When I sold Mark Robins it was on the understanding that I would be able to add to my armoury before the transfer deadline.' **(John Deehan, April 1995, after one win in 14 Premier League games)**

'Some of the football we played was frightening but everyone needs a goalscorer. It was a shame we did go down because we dictated most of our games. Norwich was the best footballing side I played in and it was a delight.' **(Mike Milligan on relegation from the Premier League, 1995)**

'I'd happily settle for winning the first four games of the season 7-6. Providing we were winning and my heart could stand it, I'd be delighted. I'd also have some fun working with the back four.' **(City manager Martin O'Neill, 1995)**

'The ball looked like a red-hot spud sometimes. If we lose games we lose in a Norwich way, passing the ball.' **(City manager Gary Megson, December 1995)**

'Mark would have been made available at the end of the season anyway.' **(Gary Megson justifies dropping Mark Bowen, one short of his 400th City appearance)**

'If the players don't play with an attitude that's 100 per cent spot on, then they might as well go and sit in the stands.' **(Gary Megson, 1996)**

'I've seen so many turning points but they've all proved false dawns.' **(Gary Megson, 1996)**

'As soon as I heard the call was from Norwich I wanted to take it. It's probably come a little bit earlier than I anticipated but it was an opportunity I could not turn down.' **(Mike Phelan becomes City's reserve team boss, but only for three months, February 1996)**

'I pick the team, I pick the shape of the team and also change it as and when I think it suits Norwich City.' **(Manager Gary Megson, 1996)**

'Three years ago Norwich were playing in Europe. Now they're staring relegation in the face. It's a travesty.' **(Jon Newsome, sold to Sheffield Wednesday, 1996)**

'It was a freak. It's a lousy way to lose a game and a lousy way to lose a local derby.' **(Gary Megson on Bryan Gunn's air kick at Ipswich, April 1996)**

'I have full control of the football side. That's some change here and that's how it should be.' **(Mike Walker returns as manager, August 1996)**

'It could have been ten, 11 or 12. It means we have problems.' **(Mike Walker after City's 5-1 defeat at West Bromwich Albion, which was swiftly followed by a 6-1 reverse at Port Vale, December 1996)**

'The game turned into a bit of a damp squid.' **(City manager Mike Walker, 1997)**

'Results don't really bother me. In fact they often tend to cloud the issue.' **(City reserve team boss Steve Foley, 1997)**

'It's suddenly going to be a difficult game because in terms of promotion and relegation, there's nothing riding on it.' **(Caretaker manager John Faulkner, May 1998)**

'When Bryan Hamilton and I are discussing the day's work in the evening we're spending a great deal more time talking about the positives than the negatives.' **(City manager Bruce Rioch, August 1998)**

'There is no player at this club that will ever take his foot off the pedal, not while I'm manager. Never.' **(Bruce Rioch after two late goals are conceded at Wigan, 1998)**

'We all thought it was going in. A sniper must have got him.' **(Bruce Rioch laments a miss by Iwan Roberts against Port Vale, October 1998)**

'Last season I would have loved to have gone to the FA Cup Final, the Worthington Cup Final and won promotion – I'm just as selfish and greedy as Alex Ferguson. But it was not to be.' **(Bruce Rioch, 1999, after City finish ninth in the First Division)**

'Playing well without the ball is an aspect of our game we've really got to work at.' **(City manager Bruce Rioch, 1999)**

'It was a bad day for us. We conceded far too many goals for our liking, but I want to give credit to the players for what they have done this season.' **(Manager Nigel Worthington after a 6-0 defeat at Fulham relegates City from the Premier League, May 2005)**

'I felt like I wanted to get away for a bit and where better to lose yourself than a place like India.' **(Craig Fleming banishes the relegation blues with a holiday, 2005)**

'It's still the biggest disappointment of my career. Not getting to the FA Cup Final with Oldham was close to it. That was a massive blow, being so close to a cup final. But the game at Fulham was an absolute disaster.' **(Craig Fleming on City's 6-0 defeat at Fulham)**

'Andy is a player that myself and the coaching staff have admired for a long while. We've had to be patient to get him, but that patience has paid off. He is a very, very good player and will be a valuable asset.' **(Nigel Worthington signs Andy Hughes, 2005)**

'They've got to keep doing the things they're asked to do rather than going off on their own fancy dan plan, which certainly cost us two points. If there had been much more time on the clock it could have cost us three points. You can't come to Southend and get complacent.' **(City manager Nigel Worthington laments a 3-3 draw at Southend, September 2006)**

'A football club is a strange place to be when you have just been relegated and players want to leave. The team spirit certainly suffered from when we went up to when we went down.' **(Darren Huckerby, 2006)**

'It's another game but it's not life or death. It's just another important game of football and we will approach it like that.' **(Caretaker manager Martin Hunter prepares for his one game in charge of City, October 2006)**

'Paul let us down badly. I'm big on discipline. I said before the game that we need every player on the pitch because we're not good enough to lose any players. I know he's come in and apologised but that's too late.' **(Peter Grant on Paul McVeigh, sent off against Cardiff, 2006)**

'Dickson's been excellent for us. He's got top, top quality, but the thing is he's got to put his working jacket on every day. If he does that he could play in the Premier League.' **(Peter Grant on Dickson Etuhu, October 2006)**

'The easy life doesn't suit me. I'm a typical Glaswegian, the first time you relax is when you're in your box, going to the big man in the sky. Yes, Norwich is a lovely part of the world but that's not the thing that excites me, it's the football club and the challenge.' **(City manager Peter Grant, November 2006)**

'I like Peter. I have a lot of time for him as a person and he's a very, very good coach who gets the best out of players and keeps players happy – and happy players can be dangerous.' **(Dion Dublin on City manager Peter Grant, 2007)**

'It's like homework to him. He comes in and gets his disk after every game to see how he can improve on everything from his fitness stats, to his passing, to the amount of ball he's given to the amount of ball he's kept. For him it's like school. You go to school, teacher gives you homework and you go away and practise.' **(Peter Grant on Dickson Etuhu, May 2007)**

'No other manager could have prepared us as well as he has done in such detail for a match situation. We have not put into practice what we've been doing in training. We've got to look at ourselves as players as we're as much to blame.' **(Darel Russell on the exit of manager Peter Grant, October 2007)**

'I've never been slow to tell someone what I think – you're not doing the job properly if you don't.' **(City assistant manager Lee Clark, 2007)**

'You tell me the last team to have just eight points in November and stay up. I've had good and bad days in football management but this is probably the best of the lot.' **(Manager Glenn Roeder hails City's survival in the Championship, May 2008)**

'Contrary to popular belief, we never had a bad day of any consequence whatever. We had plenty of good days. Every single player here occasionally gets a little bit of that temper I've got, but he's a fantastic professional. You couldn't make him have a day off. We nearly had to lock the gates to stop him coming in.' **(Glenn Roeder after releasing Darren Huckerby, May 2008)**

'We have a new staff as well as a new team this year. It has been more than a fresh lick of paint. It has been a complete redecoration. It had to be done.' **(Glenn Roeder, July 2008)**

'There was one manager I learned nothing from and that was Glenn Roeder. He made me feel like walking off the park. In general, he was an angry guy and an angry manager.' **(Former City defender Ian Murray)**

'I had a nice little phone call from Sir Alex this morning. I asked him, "What will I say?" and he just said "togetherness", and "play as a team" and that was it. It was a simple message. I just mentioned to the players that that was one of the messages I received today, from the best manager in the world.' **(Bryan Gunn after a 4-0 win over Barnsley in his first game in charge, January 2009)**

'This football club is, I think, unique. Because of the geographical position I think probably there's only Plymouth that you can compare it with.' **(John Deehan returns as chief scout, 2009)**

'We've got as much to lose as everybody else. We don't want to be part of a team that's relegated any more than the contracted players.' **(City defender Jonathan Grounds rejects the idea that loan players don't care, February 2009)**

'Mark has made a personal sacrifice for the benefit of the team because he has identified the fact that it would be a no-win situation for both of us if he took the pitch again, because of the feelings that the crowd vented towards him. He feels he just needs to make one bad pass and that's it.' **(Bryan Gunn on Mark Fotheringham's omission and loss of the captaincy, March 2009)**

'To go out on the pitch and capitulate after 30 minutes is not good enough. Those three goals were devastating.' **(Bryan Gunn after a 4-2 defeat at Charlton confirms relegation to League 1, May 2009)**

'It is the worst day, the most devastating day because of the contrast of the goodwill and hopes of thousands and thousands of fans, and the club and the community back home, and the performance on the pitch, which was intolerable. Without doubt it is the most devastating day of my long association with the club.' **(City chairman Roger Munby after a 4-2 defeat to Charlton confirms relegation to League 1, May 2009)**

'I have got a bad taste in my mouth because of the way we have gone down but at the same time I am refocusing on what I hope will be my big task of getting the club back into the Championship.' **(Bryan Gunn still hopes to stay on as manager, May 2009)**

'We've been relegated because we haven't won enough games to be out of the bottom three and I think most of the blame has to go to the 11 players who take the field.' **(City player of the season Lee Croft, 2009)**

'I am sure there will be people out there who will be for and against my appointment, but it's down to me to make sure we keep the pros as high as possible and get rid of the negatives out there. And that will only be done by results on the pitch.' **(Bryan Gunn reappointed as manager, May 2009)**

'I think that may have been a pivotal moment. That was a very important moment when, visibly, you could see the frost developing and it's very difficult to recover from that.' **(City director Michael Wynn Jones on Glenn Roeder's fall-out with fans at the 2008 annual meeting)**

'It's difficult because if you're living in Norwich, everyone you speak to keeps talking about relegation. It's hard to get it out of your head.' **(City defender Gary Doherty, 2009)**

'You see where Norwich have been in the last few years and what you hope is that they've reached rock bottom and the only way is up now.' **(Owain Tudur Jones signs for City, summer 2009)**

'With the optimism before this season with new players and the way pre-season had gone, we fell flat on our faces. People are shell-shocked and a lot of harsh words were said. It wasn't good enough, simple as that.' **(Adam Drury after the 7-1 home defeat by Colchester, August 2009)**

'We have got to apologise for what happened today, that's fair enough. But hopefully when we come back into town in the next few weeks you'll see a different team and with the 45 games we have left, there will be different scenes here.' **(Grant Holt in prophetic mood after the 7-1 home defeat by Colchester, August 2009)**

'The only thing I said to him before he took the job was, "Look, you are so well liked about the club and in this area that if you're happy doing what you've been doing in and around the club, then don't take the manager's job." Somewhere along the line, managers always get sacked.' **(Ken Brown's advice to Bryan Gunn, 2009)**

(21)

The Miracle Workers

'I still think Norwich are one of the favourites to get promoted. This result might just give them a fright.' **(Colchester manager Paul Lambert in prophetic mood after his team's 7-1 win at Carrow Road, August 2009)**

'I never had an inkling this would happen when I came here a fortnight ago. We came here and we played really, really well, but I knew enough here coming through the door that this was a huge football club. I thought at the time the result might have hurt a lot of people in this neck of the woods but never did I think I was going to come here. I just thought I was manager at Colchester.' **(Paul Lambert is appointed City boss, August 2009)**

'I still keep in contact with the gaffer. I just remember his advice when I first took over at Wycombe – he said win as many games as you can.' **(Paul Lambert on Martin O'Neill)**

'World-class, he was. I think he'll be a world-class goalkeeper, I've always thought that. For somebody who's 21, some of the saves that lad makes are extraordinary.' **(Paul Lambert on loan signing Fraser Forster)**

'We sat down and Paul Lambert said I wasn't really in his plans. He told me he was going with other players, which was fair enough. That is what managers do, but then with all the injuries we've got he just asked me in and said, "Where is your head at? I need you to play."' **(Gary Doherty, October 2009)**

'Gary has been brilliant and I'm delighted with him and for him. That decision shows how much I know about football.' **(Paul Lambert admits he wrote off Gary Doherty too soon, January 2010)**

'I keep hearing and reading comments to the effect that Norwich City should not have been in League 1 in the first place, but you are where you are in football. It is not your name that determines where you are on the ladder and whether you go up or down, otherwise every big club in the country would be in the Premier League.' **(Paul Lambert, April 2010)**

'I've always said that to perform to your best you've got to have people breathing down your neck. If you look over your shoulder and there's nobody competing with you, you become complacent and the game becomes a little bit easy. That's what I try to do, I try to put people under pressure to perform. It's not rocket science.' **(Paul Lambert, June 2010)**

'We've been told it will be very hard work during the day and very boring at night. They said you can take some laptops and DVD players but whether you'll be able to open them up and actually hold them is a different question because you'll be that tired.' **(Zak Whitbread looks forward to a pre-season tour of Germany, 2010)**

'When somebody goes up and hits a penalty, you don't know what goes through their head. You can't go up there for them and hit it. It's something he chose to do in that given moment. But while I'm at this club I don't think he'll do it again.' **(Paul Lambert on Wes Hoolahan's fluffed penalty against Preston, March 2011)**

'The lads are not thinking about anything else at the minute. Everything else in your social life and your family life is put on the back burner because it's six weeks that could change the rest of your lives. That's how big it is. The gaffer has said it's life-changing.' **(City defender Russell Martin on the promotion run-in, March 2011)**

'If I could decide what Sky want to do, then I would do it. But if you're told to play on Friday, if you're told to play on the moon, then Sky will dictate it.' **(Paul Lambert, April 2011)**

'I've enjoyed some memorable games in my career but I can't think of one better at the moment. What a game. Since I've been here and the gaffer has been here it's probably the best 90 minutes of football we have given.' **(Russell Martin on the 5-1 Championship win at Ipswich, April 2011)**

'I had my brothers there, who stripped me of my shirt and shorts. I came off in just my pants at the end.' **(Russell Martin after clinching promotion at Portsmouth, 2011)**

'I've played in every league now apart from the Premier League, from the Conference to the Championship, so I hope if I play next year that will be an unbelievable achievement for myself and one I've worked really hard for.' **(Andrew Crofts celebrates promotion, May 2011)**

'It's a miracle, an absolute miracle what has happened to this football club. The lads have done it – they deserve everything that is coming their way.' **(Paul Lambert deflects the credit for back-to-back promotions, May 2011)**

'It's the biggest night of my life so far, football or not. It's an unbelievable feeling.' **(Russell Martin on clinching promotion at Portsmouth, 2011)**

'The gaffer took the leash off the lads and said, "Just enjoy it." He knows how special an occasion it was and it was good advice. Now I'm cartwheeling. I've had a few fans come up to me and cartwheel in front of me as well.' **(Marc Tierney celebrates promotion, 2011)**

'We don't want to just be tourists in the Premier League, we want to go on and really mix it with the big boys and we think we can do that.' **(Marc Tierney, May 2011)**

'People think that she invites you round her house and bakes cakes and that kind of thing but I don't think that really happens.' **(Paul Lambert on Delia Smith, 2012)**

'I'd like to have seen him in his prime when he was 25, 26 and seen what he was like. He is one of the best one-on-one defenders that I have seen in a long while.' **(City boss Paul Lambert on Adam Drury, 2012)**

'Grant is a tough guy but a special one and I like to think there might be an England call-up if he keeps on scoring goals. I pray for all my players that they will remain healthy and strong and spiritually in a good place.' **(Lee Payne, agent for City striker Grant Holt, March 2012)**

'It was the best performance in the three years I've been here. That's the magnitude of it. It was incredible.' **(Paul Lambert after City's 2-1 win at Tottenham, Easter Monday 2012)**

'There has been a lot of hard work and Ian Culverhouse is just brilliant for me. He is a major part of what has happened. The club was close to folding. You inherit a group of lads you are not sure are good enough to get out of League 1 but you start to change the team.' **(Paul Lambert, April 2012)**

'We had to survive this season and Norwich have to survive again next season…that's what the club wants to do. I've got my own targets on what I want to do, but the club wants to survive.' **(Paul Lambert, May 2012)**

'That's five in five, which I think is some record. We can't keep continuing with that.' **(Paul Lambert is dismayed as City concede five penalties in their first five Premier League games, 2011)**

'It's a hard one to answer, that, because, as I say, I've got a contract here and everybody's doing great in their own respective jobs. We'll get this season out of the road and then I'll see what happens.' **(Paul Lambert, May 2012, asked if he will stay as City manager another season)**

'There has to be a way of managing poor results because you can't do well every single week. It's a massively difficult league to do well in.' **(City boss Chris Hughton prepares for his first season in charge, July 2012)**

'I think we got a lot of things wrong. It was a bit of a surprise for us. We had a decent pre-season and we'd looked quite solid without scoring the goals we would have liked. We didn't see that coming, I must admit.' **(City boss Chris Hughton on the 5-0 defeat at Fulham in his first game in charge)**

'I'm delighted to bring in someone of the quality of Harry. He is a very talented young player and has bags of potential.' **(Chris Hughton signs striker Harry Kane on loan from Tottenham, August 2012)**

'I've got nothing to be ashamed about, nothing. It doesn't tarnish my view because I know what we did.' **(Aston Villa boss Paul Lambert prepares to face City, October 2012)**

'I don't think it is being negative but for clubs like ourselves it is very much about trying to keep as big a gap as you can between us and going down. There is no shame in saying that. It is fact and reality for most clubs like ourselves.' **(City boss Chris Hughton, December 2012)**

'It's been getting a bit tight down there and keeps everyone entertained, but three points tomorrow and maybe people will loosen the top button on their trousers and relax a bit.' **(Russell Martin has no fear of relegation, April 2013)**

'Irrespective of the anxiety and the nervousness of certain periods, it is really just about where you finish at the end of the season. Even up to a couple of months ago, when we were having a difficult spell, most people couldn't have seen us finishing in 11th place.' **(City finish Chris Hughton's first season in charge with a 3-2 Premier League win at Manchester City)**

'It would be nice if we could scrap it. The January window is one we have got used to and it will benefit some clubs more than others if they do the right deals, but it is a disruptive period halfway through a season when as a manager all you really want to be doing is concentrating on games, preparing teams and picking up results.' **(City manager Chris Hughton, 2014)**

'I understand the situation Norwich is in. I am excited about it. Sometimes you can get comfortable if you are in a team winning every game.' **(Defender Joseph Yobo is well prepared for City's relegation battle, February 2014)**

'I was tempted to put two strikers on but what you don't want to do is give the ball away because if we'd lost we would have been relegated, virtually.' **(Manager Neil Adams defends his tactics in a 0-0 draw at Chelsea, three days before relegation is confirmed)**

'It hurts a lot for me and the players. The Premier League is the best league in the world and we have slipped out of it. Hopefully in a year we will be back in there. There is a good core group of players and, with regards the application and desire, we could not have asked for more.' **(Neil Adams accepts relegation is inevitable for City, May 2014)**

'We've had meetings, in my office and at higher levels. It's not like we don't speak to each other. His agent has been involved as well so we all know where we stand with Seb.' **(Neil Adams on the absence of Sebastien Bassong from his team, October 2014)**

'It was goals galore. We wanted to keep a clean sheet. That is not being picky but we set ourselves high standards. Today you can't criticise anything. From start to finish we totally dominated the game and the pleasing thing was not just we won but we did it in style and everyone goes home happy.' **(City boss Neil Adams enjoys a 6-1 win over Millwall in his last home game in charge, Boxing Day 2014)**

'I'm confident and every time the ball is coming to me at the moment I'm hitting it and it's going in. And that's the motto I grew up with. If you don't shoot you don't score. It's paying off for me – and I'm not going to stop shooting.' **(City player of the season Bradley Johnson explains his 15 Championship goals, May 2015)**

'There is nothing worse than turning up with six games to go in a season and nothing to play for and you are plodding through. You want to be part of the games that really matter, when emotions are running high and people are getting stuck in.' **(City boss Alex Neil prepares for the play-offs, May 2015)**

'It's a special day, it turned out to be our day but I thought we were magnificent from start to finish. The way we started was strong, we were snapping at tackles, we got the ball moving, we played some brilliant stuff, the tactics were spot on.' **(Striker Cameron Jerome, goalscorer in the Championship play-off final, May 2015)**

'To lead a team out at Wembley, and then lead them up the steps to pick up the trophy, it's the proudest moment of my career and I don't think it'll be topped. It feels amazing. To do it the way we've done it is the ultimate. It tops everything we've done at this football club for me, since I've been here.' **(Russell Martin leads City to Wembley victory, May 2015)**

'It takes bottle to come to a play-off final and perform because every week in the Championship we were reminded of the pressure, we were the best squad and should go up. To carry that and have that dodgy spell and pick it up and drive it home, come here and not be denied, speaks volumes.' **(City manager Alex Neil on promotion, May 2015)**

'We are just bowled over by him. He is incredible. He is a lovely man, he's intelligent, self-confident and he doesn't have an ego – and that's quite hard.' **(Delia Smith has the last word on manager Alex Neil)**

(22)

Time To Say Goodbye

'For some time past I have not been able to shut my eyes to the fact that my services to Norwich City have not been appreciated in the manner in which I expected them to be.' **(John Bowman's letter of resignation as City manager, June 1907)**

'I didn't know too much about my move to Tottenham. I was only told about it on the Thursday and by the Saturday I had to travel up to play with all these great stars around me. I was a shy boy and played fewer than 50 games for Norwich, but then I had to plonk myself down alongside people like Danny Blanchflower.' **(Maurice Norman, Norwich centre-half, then Tottenham double winner)**

'There has been criticism of the fact that I let so many players go at the end of last season. Of Brennan I can only say that I firmly believed, and still do, that in spite of his undoubted ability he was not a player to bring out the best in his colleagues.' **(City manager Tom Parker defends releasing Bobby Brennan, who briefly joined non-league Great Yarmouth, 1956)**

'Macaulay said he'd go to another club and then told me the terms that had been offered to him. That was one of the reasons why he wanted to be released.' **(City chairman Geoffrey Watling loses his manager to West Bromwich Albion and an era ends, October 1961)**

'Norwich had a reputation for being a tough board to work for. The offer came from Cardiff and I thought I would try my luck there. It was not a difficult decision mainly because of the chairman. I was just glad to get away.' **(George Swindin, City manager for just 20 matches)**

'It is clear from the serious fall in attendances that the club has not been providing entertainment adequate to attract supporters and this public disappointment is shared by the board. After considering the position fully the directors have arrived at the conclusion that the playing resources require a new approach. To this end we have decided with regret to terminate the contract of the manager.' **(Geoffrey Watling confirms the sacking of manager Lol Morgan, April 1969)**

'It was a new beginning for the club but it turned out a bitter-sweet experience for me because I never had the chance to show what I could do in the First Division. It wasn't how I wanted it to end. I was a little bit miffed, you could say.' **(Promotion winner Ken Foggo makes a sad exit, 1973)**

'Dear Mr Chairman, following our conversation following today's game, please accept my resignation. Yours sincerely, R. Saunders.' **(City manager Ron Saunders marks his exit with 17 handwritten words, 1973)**

'I suggested I would wait until Monday morning before opening the letter, to give him time to reconsider, but he wouldn't hear of it. The resignation came as a complete surprise to all of us in view of the fact that Mr Saunders' contract has over three years to run.' **(City chairman Arthur South reacts to Ron Saunders's exit, 1973)**

'In all my career I had never imagined myself at Wembley, and here was the chance. But I had to look at the long-term future, so I decided to take the Bournemouth job. It was too good to let it go.' **(John Benson opts for management ahead of a possible Wembley final appearance, 1975)**

'I was only 22 when I left Norwich, but when the chance came to go to America I thought I might never get it again. Some of the greatest players in the world were out there like Beckenbauer, Pele, Cruyff and Neeskens and it was a boom time for soccer in America.' **(City striker Roger Gibbins)**

'I didn't get the opportunity I hoped for. That was the manager's choice. An FA Cup tie against Orient was my only full game and I had a few minutes as a substitute at Newcastle. But the way I left did not sour my memories of Norwich in any way. I loved the place. I was a young man at my first club and just wanted to play football. I was living the dream.' **(Defender Jim Fleeting on his brief first-team career with City)**

'Going to Newcastle was the worst decision I ever made. The manager told me they were hard up for cash and I was the only one he could sell.' **(Full-back Ian Davies)**

'It was a bit of a wrench to leave, to be honest, because I turned down Manchester City the first time. I didn't want to go. But when they came back in the second time around, it was a lot of money for the club, and so I went.' **(Kevin Reeves recalls his £1m move to Manchester City)**

'We were playing a youth game here on a Wednesday evening and I was just getting ready when John Bond came round to my house. He offered me the job to go with him as assistant at Manchester City and we shook hands on the deal. Then after the youth game Sir Arthur South offered me the job as manager here. I couldn't say anything. I was so dumbfounded. It was a difficult one but I'd shaken hands on it with John.' **(John Benson on his second exit from City, 1980)**

'That's it. I'm off. There is nothing here for me now. They have a caretaker coach and I have a job at Manchester City.' **(First team coach John Sainty joins the exodus to Manchester City, 1980)**

'I am sorry he wants to leave but blood is thicker than water. He is a good boy, a good son and a good footballer and if Manchester City want to come in for him, we won't stand in his way.' **(Sir Arthur South grants Kevin Bond a transfer, November 1980)**

'I was aware that other clubs were interested but Brian Clough impressed me. He is obviously a winner and makes those around him winners too. Certain moves have to be made in life and I hope I've made the right one.' **(Justin Fashanu joins Nottingham Forest for £1m, August 1981)**

'Everybody seems to be asking me that at the moment as if I am going to finish in a couple of weeks. My intention is to play for a lot longer and hopefully with Norwich in the First Division.' **(Full-back Willie Donachie before the last of his 14 games for City, December 1981)**

'I'm joining a rat race for football jobs with a great many others. Something has got to be done at the top level to prevent football being buried. It really is a frightening thought. I have a wife and kids and a mortgage so I've got to start looking.’ **(John McDowell loses his job as City reserve team coach, March 1982)**

‘I didn’t play all that well and when John Bond left that was it, really.’ **(Clive Woods on his 37 appearances for City)**

‘When I re-signed for Norwich I took a £400 per week drop in pay which I was promised would be put right in 18 months. I had no desire to leave but it was a matter of principle.’ **(Martin O’Neill leaves City for the second time, 1983)**

‘I don’t really think I’ll go back into the professional game. I’m really enjoying my football now playing for Poringland on Saturdays, Hobbies on Sundays and J J Fun City on Thursdays.’ **(Richard Symonds after being released by City, 1984)**

‘Me and Ken Brown, who I love dearly, had our first little falling out and me being a bit strong-willed, I said that was it.’ **(Keith Bertschin leaves City for Stoke, 1984)**

‘I got fed up being made a scapegoat when things went wrong. I was already upset at being left out at Wembley. That was what I had spent ten years at Norwich waiting for but when it happened I was not part of it. It was so disappointing. I always gave everything I had to the club but Norwich didn’t seem bothered whether I stayed or left.’ **(Greg Downs joins Coventry, July 1985)**

‘I didn’t expect to be used as bait.’ **(John Deehan joins Ipswich in a swap deal for Trevor Putney, 1986)**

‘As one door closed, another one slammed in my face.’ **(Striker David Hodgson on leaving Norwich for Jerez, 1987)**

'If I have let anyone down I apologise. I don't want to appear big-headed but perhaps it is Norwich's loss more than mine.' **(Ken Brown, sacked as manager, 1987)**

'I'd had links with that club going back 40 years and I loved the place. When I went home that night I sat in my garden looking into the pond. I suffered a great deal after being finished in that manner after 40 years.' **(Ronnie Brooks on being axed as City chief scout, 1986)**

'I have reached the stage in my career where I have to be looking to be a number one. I have served my apprenticeship here and hopefully someone will recognise my ability and give me the opportunity.' **(Mel Machin resigns as City chief coach, May 1987)**

"It is a big wrench leaving after so long. The hardest part was saying goodbye to the players. Working with them day in and day out, you are bound to get a bit close to them. There were one or two lumps in my throat" **(Mel Machin, May 1987)**

'For a little while after I left I don't think I was very popular but I think they realise that you have to go when Manchester United are calling.' **(Steve Bruce)**

'The matter of Ken's enforced departure was quite unnecessarily brutal.' **(Nick Butcher, solicitor, defends sacked boss Brown, 1988)**

'I left Norwich because I wasn't getting a regular place, plus I was offered a few quid to go to Leicester. I thought probably I was a young kid who thought he knew it all and went for gold, really, instead of football. I wish I'd never left Norwich.' **(Tony Spearing)**

'When I was dropped I think it was inevitable I had to go. It was not correct I had an attitude problem. I never let

Norwich City down. That tarnished my image.' **(Robert Rosario joins Coventry, 1991)**

'If they are going to pay peanuts then I'm off.' **(David Phillips leaves City for Nottingham Forest, 1993)**

'I feel I was forced to make a decision and I am happy with it because I knew what I wanted. I am ambitious. If I get things right here, the sky is the limit.' **(Manager Mike Walker quits City for Everton, 1994)**

'He did not speak to me or any of his staff or his players and that is disappointing. I'm surprised he walked out the day before an important game but these things happen and we have to live with them.' **(Robert Chase on manager Mike Walker's exit to Everton, January 1994)**

'I know it's going to be "Chase out! Chase out!" but he's been super to me. I think he's always got the players' interests at heart.' **(Ruel Fox moves to Newcastle for £2.25m, 1994)**

'We find that Everton indirectly induced Mike Walker to terminate his contract of employment with Norwich and indirectly approached him.' **(FA Premier League tribunal fines Everton £75,000 plus £50,000 costs, 1994)**

'My main concern is to go to a club where I can improve my game. Money is not my god.' **(Chris Sutton, July 1994)**

'I wanted to sell Chris Sutton like a hole in the head.' **(Robert Chase, July 1994)**

'It was a big step down when I went from Norwich to Bradford. I won't say it wasn't. Two of the last games

I played for Norwich were in the San Siro and at Old Trafford.' **(Lee Power, 1995)**

'It was a day I hoped would never happen, a day I hoped would pass me by. But I had to face reality. I wasn't enjoying the job any more.' **(John Deehan resigns as City manager, April 1995)**

'I was going home and not sleeping because I was trying to come up with the answer to an equation that was unanswerable – how to help a young side stay in the Premiership with no money.' **(John Deehan)**

'It would be untrue to say the position at Leicester didn't have some bearing on my decision to leave Norwich.' **(Martin O'Neill after resigning as manager, 1995)**

'My annoyance is I left the club and broke a contract, the only one I have ever broken.' **(Martin O'Neill)**

'For the last two months, Martin hasn't been the Martin I know.' **(Paul Franklin, assistant to Martin O'Neill, December 1995)**

'I was disappointed to leave but Mr Chase made it perfectly clear that Ashley Ward and I were going.' **(Jon Newsome, sold to Sheffield Wednesday, 1996)**

'Football is not the main issue at Norwich at the moment and the pressure on the players is unbelievable. It's a cracking club and the fans deserve better.' **(Striker Ashley Ward is sold to Derby for £1m, March 1996)**

'Thanks to you all and goodbye.' **(Robert Chase sells his shares to Geoffrey Watling and steps down from the board, May 1996)**

'It is an opportunity I can't turn down. It was nothing detrimental about the offer here but the money is a big, big part of it and it's a great opportunity, especially at my age.' **(Ian Crook turns down an extra year with City to join Sanfrecce Hiroshima, 1997)**

'Mutual consent? Cobblers. The board is insulting our intelligence.' **(Columnist Man in the Stands on Mike Walker's sacking, 1998)**

'There is ambition in the club but you do need the resources on occasions to attain those ambitions. That was the major part of the decision I have taken.' **(Bruce Rioch resigns as City boss, March 2000)**

'He is without doubt one of the most honest and principled people I have come across in my 26 years in football.' **(Gordon Bennett on Bruce Rioch's resignation, March 2000)**

'We've had five years of total mediocrity at Norwich City.' **(Manager Bryan Hamilton, just before resigning, 2000)**

'If I had had the time to make the changes I wanted and bring players in it would have been different.' **(Bryan Hamilton, who made 14 signings in nine months as City manager, 2000)**

'It was all down to a hard core of disaffected fans and a hostile press. I'm not the sort to hang around when I feel unwanted, even by a smallish group with undue influence.' **(Bryan Hamilton resigns as City boss, December 2000)**

'I think a lot of harsh things were written, things that shouldn't have been mentioned and written about the manager, which was diabolical.' **(Acting manager Nigel**

Worthington defends predecessor Bryan Hamilton, December 2000)

'It was a situation we had to deal with and both parties are happy.' **(Manager Nigel Worthington on a reported £200,000 pay-off to Steve Walsh, whose 129 minutes of first team action with City cost £1,500 per minute)**

'It was coming up to the time for a new contract, Nigel had only been in charge a few weeks, the transfer window closed in March and it came about I had this chance to go to Leicester. I was 22 and I thought it was too good an opportunity to miss.' **(Lee Marshall, 2007)**

'I understand they are going to be upset. I had 16 great years there, but I wanted to leave and when I looked at my options Ipswich Town was the best one. When I knew Ipswich were interested there wasn't much doubt about where I wanted to go. In my first year at Ipswich I've got the chance of playing Premiership football and European football.' **(City goalkeeper Andy Marshall crosses the border, July 2001)**

'I was definitely led up the garden path. As far as I knew, I was playing in the team, I thought I was playing well, I got my new contract and all of a sudden I wasn't playing.' **(Adrian Forbes is sold to Luton four months after agreeing a new contract, July 2001)**

'It got to the stage where myself and Nigel did not see eye to eye and there was only ever going to be one winner. Towards the end, I didn't look forward to going to training at Colney, so when the chance to move to Oldham came about I was glad to go.' **(Simon Charlton, 2006)**

'My team will live to fight another day and I intend to live to fight another day as well.' **(Nigel Worthington, October 2006, minutes before being sacked)**

'The day I walk out of this door, whether it's good, bad, indifferent, getting the sack, moving on, I want people to go away and say he was true to his word and stood by his guns.' **(City manager Peter Grant, July 2007, three months before his exit)**

'The manager at Norwich told me he didn't want me to leave, but I didn't want to stay and be a squad player.' **(Andy Hughes joins Leeds, August 2007)**

'Unfortunately, I feel that the balls haven't bounced the right way for me over the last 12 months. I have had fantastic support from the board from minute one right up until the time of leaving, but we are in a results-driven business and I don't like being second best at anything.' **(Peter Grant steps down as City manager, October 2007)**

'I tried to play in the Championship, but with the unhappy start to the season and with the change in manager, I now need to re-start my career back in Prague.' **(Czech striker David Strihavka leaves City after six months and one goal, January 2008)**

'In between the ages of 15 and 17, I worked in an ice cream factory, in a hosiery factory, in a leisure centre, and I played for non-league clubs in and around Leicestershire and I know what it's like not to be a footballer. I know what it's like to work 60 hours, 70 hours and get £80 a week. I know what it's like to go to work on a moped with a big backpack on. So being a footballer so long has made me appreciate how lucky footballers in general are. Being a footballer as a male person is the best job in the world.' **(Dion Dublin prepares for his final game for City at Sheffield Wednesday, 2008)**

'Apart from being a top footballer, Dion is a top human being with lots of humility. He's my type of person and lots of others as well. I just hope he has a happy retirement.' **(Glenn Roeder on Dion Dublin, May 2008)**

'They've not spoken to me at all. In the next week it's got to be done but, like I say, I'm not a YTS lad. It's a bit strange that I'm having to wait but that's how it goes.' **(Darren Huckerby, out of contract, awaits his fate after 4-1 defeat at Sheffield Wednesday, May 2008)**

'I feel it should have been done so I could say my farewells to the fans and the people who have meant so much to me over the years. It feels like I've been cheated of that, really. But apart from that, it's been a great five years. It's a strange feeling. Cleaning out my locker today was odd, especially seeing Dion do it five minutes before me. It's difficult but that's football. The club comes first and it always will do.' **(Darren Huckerby is released by manager Glenn Roeder, May 2008)**

'It was a tough call. It wasn't a decision that was made easily – or quickly…things that he did here were quite amazing for the club, but Darren Huckerby would never, ever expect to be a player that was in the team, out of the team. And I think there comes a time for certain players – and Darren would be one of those – that if you're not going to be in the first couple of names on the team sheet then perhaps it is time to move on.' **(Glenn Roeder explains why he released Darren Huckerby, May 2008)**

'To get this award in front of such great players means a lot. But these things come to an end and it's time for the club to move forward. All these great players had to move on and it's time for me to do so.' **(Darren Huckerby named in the Greatest Ever XI, May 2008)**

'I'm on what they call gardening leave these days. The only problem is I haven't got a garden.' **(Ex-City defender Rob Newman loses his job at Bournemouth, 2008)**

'Lee has been itching to become a manager. He's very ambitious. I like ambitious people, and I don't want to work with people who have no ambition to improve themselves in life.' **(Glenn Roeder loses assistant boss Lee Clark to Huddersfield, December 2008)**

'We've taken the club down. It's not as if there are boys in there, superstars who are going to get good moves when they're getting relegated. So we just have to plug on. I have no problem staying here because I don't think there are clubs lining up for any of the boys when we've just had 46 games to stay in the Championship and got relegated.' **(City goalkeeper David Marshall, nine days before joining Cardiff City, May 2009)**

'Lee has made it clear that he will want to move on to pastures new. As the Barry Butler Player of the Year, somebody who the fans respected this season and voted for, it's an unfortunate scenario. I suppose, as a football club, we should wish Lee all the best in his future.' **(City manager Bryan Gunn bids farewell to Lee Croft, May 2009)**

'No, it's a stupid question. I don't doubt my position.' **(City manager Bryan Gunn, six days before being sacked, August 2009)**

'I think it's extremely unfair me being linked with Aston Villa when they've got a really good manager up there and they're trying everything they can to stay in the league. It's unfair for me to say anything on that.' **(Paul Lambert, 27 April 2012)**

'Being associated with the club for so many years has given me so many life experiences and brought out every emotion possible, from the highest to the lowest. It has been an incredible journey. But all things come to an end and it's time for me to move on. The club is about today and tomorrow, not what people have done in the past.' **(Jeremy Goss loses his role as City's community ambassador, 2010)**

'I'm delighted I am at Norwich if that's what you're asking me. I have never said I wanted away. Not a thing have I said and people jump to conclusions.' **(Paul Lambert, 22 May 2012, eight days before resigning as manager)**

'I had three brilliant years there, but I am now probably the worst manager in the club's history because I have left. I'm sure the fans are a little hurt that I have gone, but that is all I will say on the matter. I had my reasons to leave but I gave Norwich City everything I had. I had my reasons and they were good reasons.' **(Paul Lambert on his resignation as manager, 2012)**

'Paul has already earned his place in Norwich City Football Club history and, no matter what happens, will always have a friendly welcome at Carrow Road.' **(Club statement confirms Paul Lambert's resignation as manager, June 2012)**

'What we have to make sure is that this result does not drain the confidence. I understand the frustration of the crowd and we just have to get on with it.' **(Chris Hughton after a 1-0 defeat by West Bromwich Albion, the day before being sacked as manager, April 2014)**

'I understand the recent frustrations, but I remained totally confident that we were on course to create history at the club by retaining our top-flight status and move into a fourth consecutive season in the Premier League.' **(Chris Hughton after being sacked, April 2014)**

'I firmly believe that we are still on course for a crack at promotion back to the Premier League. That is where this club belongs. However, I feel it is in the best interests of the team that an immediate change is made in order to ensure a positive impact on results.' **(Neil Adams resigns as City manager, January 2015)**

Norfolk-born David Cuffley spent nearly 30 years on the sports desk of the *Eastern Daily Press* and *Norwich Evening News*, including 13 seasons covering Norwich City and more than a decade as *Evening News* sports editor. He reported on the Canaries' rollercoaster fortunes in a period that included their first European tie, two FA Cup semi-finals, the drop into League One and Paul Lambert's stirring promotion double. A lifelong Norwich fan, he was a member of the BBC *Songs of Praise* FA Cup Fans' Choir chosen to sing 'Abide With Me' before the 2015 FA Cup Final at Wembley.